Really learn

100

phrasal verbs for business

OXFORD
UNIVERSITY PRESS

OXFORD
UNIVERSITY PRESS

Great Clarendon Street, Oxford OX2 6DP

Oxford University Press is a department of the University of Oxford.
It furthers the University's objective of excellence in research, scholarship,
and education by publishing worldwide in

Oxford New York

Auckland Cape Town Dar es Salaam Hong Kong Karachi
Kuala Lumpur Madrid Melbourne Mexico City Nairobi
New Delhi Shanghai Taipei Toronto

With offices in

Argentina Austria Brazil Chile Czech Republic France Greece
Guatemala Hungary Italy Japan Poland Portugal Singapore
South Korea Switzerland Thailand Turkey Ukraine Vietnam

OXFORD and OXFORD ENGLISH are registered trade marks of
Oxford University Press in the UK and in certain other countries

The British National Corpus is a collaborative project involving Oxford
University Press, Longman, Chambers, the Universities of Oxford and
Lancaster and the British Library

ISBN: 978 0 19 431696 5

Edited by Dilys Parkinson
Assisted by Ben Francis

Printed in China

Contents

How to use **Really learn 100 phrasal verbs for business**

This book contains 100 of the most frequently used phrasal verbs in the world of business. Each verb is presented on a single page, with examples and exercises that are designed to show both the meaning and the situations in which it is most commonly used. Although some of the verbs have several meanings, only those that are directly connected with work and business have been included.

How the book is organized

The phrasal verbs are arranged in alphabetical order. Each page can be studied on its own so you can look at the pages in any order that you find useful or interesting. The answers to the exercises can be found in the KEY TO THE EXERCISES at the back of the book. There are also ten REVIEW pages in the middle of the book in which the phrasal verbs are presented in groups for further study and revision. The answers to the exercises on these pages are at the end of the REVIEW section.

How the pages are arranged

↓ **Title**

> # 9 **break** something **down** (**into** something)

This shows you the general form of the phrasal verb as well as giving you some important grammatical information. For example, you can see that the verb

shown above can be used with an object and that the object is a thing rather than a person. *Break something down into something* can also be used.

↓ **Study**

> **Study** Read these sentences carefully.
> ▸ I have **broken** the sales figures **down** into regions.
> ▸ The software **breaks down** the results by time and frequency.
> ▸ The job's easier if you **break** it **down** into smaller tasks.
> ▸ The data **was broken down** into six different categories.

This section contains examples of the phrasal verb as it is used in real contexts. It is important to study this section as the examples provide information both about the grammar of the verb and the words that it is frequently used with.

↓ **Check**

> ### Check
>
> Use the sentences in the Study box to help you do these exercises.
>
> **MEANING**
>
> If you **break something down**, do you:
>
> **a** reduce its price so that it is very cheap?
> **b** destroy it by cutting it into small pieces?
> **c** divide it into smaller pieces so that it is easier to do or understand?
>
> **GRAMMAR**
>
> Which of these are grammatically possible?
>
> **a** I will break down the sales results.
> **b** I will break them down.
> **c** I will break down them.
> **d** The sales results broke down.
> **e** The sales results were broken down.
>
> → Check your answers in the key

- **Meaning**: When you do these exercises, remember to look back at the example sentences in the STUDY section because these will help you to understand the meaning.

- **Grammar**: In this section you must try to decide which sentences are correct or incorrect in terms of their grammatical structure. Remember that all the possible grammatical structures are presented in the STUDY section.

It is important to check your answers to the MEANING and GRAMMAR exercises before you move on to the next section.

↓ **Practise**

> ## Practise
>
> **1** Match the two halves to make complete sentences
>
> | | | | |
> |---|---|---|---|
> | **a** | The economy can be broken down into | **i** | 6 different departments. |
> | **b** | The structure of the company is broken down into | **ii** | separate tasks to see how busy she is. |
> | **c** | If you break production costs down in | **iii** | the report, we can see the problem. |
> | **d** | He broke the project down into | **iv** | sectors according to the type of industry. |
> | **e** | Let's break the PA's duties down into | **v** | several stages. |
>
> **2** Read the text and find and underline *two* verbs that could be replaced by a form of **break down**. Then correct and rewrite the sentences below the text using a form of **break down**.
>
> > Henry Ford's most famous car was the Model T. In order to make this car, he invented a new system of production: the assembly line. On Ford's assembly line, the manufacture of a car was divided into 84 simple tasks each done by a different worker. By separating out production in this way, he was able to speed up production and reduce labour costs. In the process, he started a revolution in manufacturing.
>
> **a** On an assembly line, production is divided into a few complex tasks.
>
> _____
>
> **b** Ford separated the production of the Model T into 54 tasks.
>
> _____
>
> → Check your answers in the key

This section contains exercises that give you practice in using the phrasal verbs in typical contexts. If you have difficulty with any of the exercises, look back at the **Study** and **Check** sections for help. Again, after completing the exercises, you should check your answers carefully.

↓ **Build your vocabulary**

> ## Build your vocabulary
>
> RELATED WORDS   NOUN: **a breakdown** (= division of something larger into smaller parts.) (This noun is usually singular)
> > ▸ *Can you give me a **breakdown** of the sales figures by Monday?*

This gives extra information about the phrasal verb. For **break something down**, you are given information on RELATED WORDS.

Categories in the **Build your vocabulary** section include:

- **Related words:** this tells you about words formed from the phrasal verb.
- **Other meanings:** other useful meanings that the phrasal verb may have.

- **Synonyms:** verbs that have the same meaning.
- **Opposites:** other verbs that have the opposite meaning.
- **Similar verbs:** other verbs with a similar meaning.

1 account for something

Study Read these sentences carefully.

- ▸ Our fashion division **accounts for** about 35% of sales.
- ▸ Our oil and gas business, which accounts for 30 000 staff and $6 billion in revenue, will be sold next year.
- ▸ Wages **accounted for** less than half of the budget.
- ▸ 95% of our revenues can be **accounted for** by 25% of our customers.

Check

Use the sentences in the Study box to help you do these exercises.

MEANING

Which of these best matches this meaning of **account for something**?

a to get someone to do your business accounts

b to spend a particular amount of money

c to form or be the source of a particular amount of something

GRAMMAR

Which of these are grammatically possible?

a Overseas orders accounted for 25% of our sales.

b Overseas orders are accounted for 25% of our sales.

c 25% of our sales are accounted for by overseas orders.

→ Now check your answers in the key.

Practise

1 Rewrite the following sentences so that the meaning stays the same, using the correct form of **account for something**.

a Students form about 10% of our customers.

 Students _____

b 28% of jobs in the region are manufacturing jobs.

 28% of jobs _____

2 Look at the information below about the number of managers in a company. Then answer the questions using the correct form of **account for something**.

	1970	2005
Total number of managers in the company	30	40
Women managers in the company	3	10

a What % of managers were men in 1970?

 _____

b What % of managers are men in 2005?

 _____

c What % of managers were women in 1970?

 _____

d What % of managers are women in 2005?

 _____

→ Now check your answers in the key.

Build your vocabulary

OTHER MEANINGS **Account for something** can also mean 'to record an amount in a company's financial records in a particular way':

- ▸ *The capital gain has **been accounted for** in the profit and loss account.*

2 back something up

Study Read these sentences carefully.

▶ I **back up** all my files on CD-ROM once a week.
▶ If you have important files on your PC, you must **back** them **up**.
▶ How do I **back** my computer's hard drive **up**?
▶ Make sure data is **backed up** regularly.

Check

Use the sentences in the Study box to help you do these exercises.

MEANING

Choose the best meaning of
back something up:

a to move a file, program, etc. to a
   different place on a computer
b to make a second copy of a file,
   program, etc. to use if the main
   one fails

GRAMMAR

Which of these are grammatically possible?

a I backed up my files.
b I backed my files up.
c I backed up them.
d I backed them up.
e My files were backed up.

→ Now check your answers in the key.

Practise

1 Put these words in the correct order to make a sentence:

a you backed the have data up?
b hard drive it I up on the backed
c forgot to up I back it

2 Rewrite the *italic* part of each sentence using **back up** and an object (noun or
pronoun) and any other words you need:

a I lost all my work because I hadn't *saved it on the hard drive.*

_____

b You can *save all your folders* or just individual documents.

_____

c *Saving data* is one of the basics of any computer system.

_____

d You should always remember *to save your work* on the C-drive.

_____

→ Now check your answers in the key.

Build your vocabulary

RELATED WORDS   NOUN: **backup** (This noun is countable.)

▶ *Have you made **backups** of your files?*
▶ *a **backup** disk*

3 bail somebody or something out (of something)

- ▶ The government has refused to **bail** the company **out** again.
- ▶ Private business helped to **bail out** the museum.
- ▶ We couldn't get any cash from our parent company to **bail** us **out**.
- ▶ A $40 million government loan **bailed** the industry **out** of financial crisis.
- ▶ The airline had to be **bailed out** by the government.

Check

Use the sentences in the Study box to help you do these exercises.

MEANING

Complete the meaning of **bail somebody or something out** using the words below:

difficulties	financial	rescue

to _____ a person or an

organization from _____ ,

especially _____ difficulties

GRAMMAR

Which of these are grammatically possible?

- a The government bailed the company out.
- b The government bailed it out.
- c The government bailed out the company.
- d The government bailed out of it.
- e The company was bailed out by the government.

→ Now check your answers in the key.

Practise

1 Complete these sentences using a form of **bail out (of)** and one of the words or phrases from the list below.

it	them	loss-making companies	by its shareholders	the football club

- a When banks go bust, the government usually _____
- b A millionaire fan has offered to _____
- c The company has been in trouble before but this time the government will not

  _____

- d The telecoms company was _____
- e The state will not be able to go on _____

2 Discussion: In recent years, several national airlines have had financial problems which have been solved by governments bailing them out. Some people think that governments should not bail out airlines or other companies that are in difficulty. What is your opinion?

→ Now check your answers in the key.

Build your vocabulary

RELATED WORDS NOUN: **bailout** (This is a countable noun.)
- ▶ *The company has received a $5 billion government **bailout**.*

SIMILAR VERBS **shore something up**:
- ▶ *State aid was used to **shore up** failing businesses.*

→ **prop something up** on page 65

4 beat off somebody or something

▸ The company has **beaten off** strong competition from abroad.
▸ We succeeded in **beating off** a hostile takeover bid.
▸ There were six other candidates for the job, but she **beat** them all **off**.
▸ A challenge from a rival company was **beaten off**.

Check

Use the sentences in the Study box to help you do these exercises.

MEANING

Which of the following means the same as **beat off somebody or something**?

a to attack somebody
b to defeat somebody in a
   competition for something
c to send information quickly to
   somebody

GRAMMAR

Which of these are grammatically possible?

a They beat off strong competition.
b They beat off it.
c They beat it off.
d Strong competition was beaten off.

→ Now check your answers in the key.

Practise

1 Match the two halves to make complete sentences.

a He had beaten off some good
   candidates…
b The modelling agency beat off
   stiff competition…
c The software firm has beaten off
   several big companies…
d They will have difficulty beating off…

i   to get the star onto their books.

ii challenges from foreign car makers

iii to win the contract for a new
    IT system.
iv to get the job.

2 Complete these sentences with the correct form of **beat off**:

a We won the contract after _____
   seven other companies.

b In order to retain their market share, British companies
   have to _____ cheap foreign imports.

c They have _____ fierce competition
   from rival bidders.

→ Now check your answers in the key.

Build your vocabulary

SYNONYMS The verb **fight off somebody or something** can be used in the same way:
▸ *The company has successfully **fought off** a hostile takeover bid.*

5 be down; be up

Study Read these sentences carefully.

▸ Profits **are down** by 6%.
▸ The number of businesses that failed **is down** from 8 000 last year to 6 500.
▸ Manufacturing productivity **is up** by 20%.
▸ The euro **was** slightly **up** in relation to the dollar.
▸ People think that the price of air travel **will be up** this year.

Check

Use the sentences in the Study box to help you do these exercises.

MEANING
Profits, *sales* and *prices* can **be down** or
be up. Can you think of three more
things that can **be down** or **be up**?

_____

_____

_____

GRAMMAR
Which of these are grammatically possible?

a Prices are down.
b Prices are being down.
c Prices were down.
d Prices are up.
e Prices will be up.

→ Now check your answers in the key.

Practise

1 Choose the correct form of **be down** or **be up** to fill in the gaps in the sentences.

| is up   be up   are down   were down by   are up |

a It has been a good year and profits _____ by 7.5%

b Sales _____ 9% last year.

c The forecast is that profits will _____ this year.

d Unemployment _____ for the third year running.

e Interest rates _____ .

2 Rewrite the following newspaper headlines so that the meaning stays the
same, using a form of **be down** or **be up**.

a | PROFITS IN THE AIRLINE INDUSTRY HAVE DECREASED BY 7%

_____

b | COMPANY SALES ARE 7% HIGHER

_____

c | SHARE PRICES ARE NOW LOWER

_____

→ Now check your answers in the key.

Build your vocabulary

SIMILAR VERBS → **go down, go up** on page 41

6 bottom out

- The fall in sales is beginning to **bottom out**.
- The market has **bottomed out** and share prices are rising again.
- The recession is **bottoming out**, which is good for industry.

Check

Use the sentences in the Study box to help you do these exercises.

MEANING

Use *two* of the words below to help you complete the meaning of **bottom out**.

worse   lowest   better   highest

If markets, prices or bad situations **bottom out**, they reach their _____ point and then stop getting _____ .

→ Now check your answers in the key.

GRAMMAR

Which of these are grammatically possible?

a Prices will soon bottom themselves out.
b Prices will soon bottom out.
c An increase in demand will soon bottom out prices.

Practise

1 Read this piece of text and then answer the questions about it.

In a number of European countries, the ratio of workers to non-workers fell from the early 1950s onwards and bottomed out in the mid-1970s. Then it rose gradually as the baby boomers (people born when a lot of babies were born) reached working age and the average family size fell.

a When did the ratio of workers to non-workers start falling? _____

b When did the ratio of workers to non-workers stop falling? _____

c Why did the ratio of workers to non-workers start rising again?

_____

2 Rewrite the words in *italic*, using an appropriate form of **bottom out**:

a The share price *reached its lowest point* at $5.45.

_____

b Sales are *beginning to stop falling*.

_____

→ Now check your answers in the key.

Build your vocabulary

SIMILAR VERBS   → **level off** on page 53

Level off/out and **flatten out** both mean to stop falling but unlike **bottom out** they can *also* mean to stop rising:
- *Sales are beginning to **flatten out** as we reach saturation point.*

OPPOSITES   **To peak** (to reach the highest point):
- *Sales **peaked** in March last year and have fallen steadily since then.*

7 branch out (into something)

Study Read these sentences carefully.
- ▸ The travel company has **branched out** and bought its own hotels.
- ▸ Bookstores are **branching out** into new areas such as CDs and gifts.
- ▸ He wanted to **branch out** from accounting into marketing.
- ▸ She decided to **branch out** on her own and start a new company.

Check

Use the sentences in the Study box to help you do these exercises.

MEANING

If a company or person **branches out**, what do they do? Choose *one* answer.

a join together with another company
b do less work than they normally do
c start doing different work from the work they normally do

GRAMMAR

Which of these are grammatically possible?

a The company branched out.
b The company is branching out into furniture.
c They branched out the company.
d She branched out on her own.

→ Now check your answers in the key.

Practise

1 Read the following text and then fill the gaps in the sentences using the correct form of **branch out (into something)**.

Business wasn't going well so we knew we had to make some changes. After much discussion we decided to start selling videos and DVDs too. You have to be careful when you start selling other things because customers need to know that you will still offer the same high level of service.

a For business reasons we decided to _____ selling videos and DVDs.

b If you _____ , you need to be careful that customers still know your service is good.

2 Rewrite the following sentences so that the meaning stays the same, using the correct form of **branch out (into something)**:

a We have now started making sportswear.

_____

b Profits were falling until we decided to sell computer games as well.

_____

c I have worked for the company for ten years and I would like to start my own business.

_____

→ Now check your answers in the key.

Build your vocabulary

SYNONYMS A company can also **diversify (into something)**:
- ▸ *They have **diversified** into new areas to increase their overseas business.*

8 break down

▶ Trade talks sometimes **break down** over the issue of import duty.
▶ The deal has **broken down** so we will have to look for another partner.
▶ The discussions **broke down** without any agreement between the two sides.
▶ This is the latest example of a TV sports deal **breaking down**.

Check

Use the sentences in the Study box to help you do these exercises.

MEANING

If talks and discussions **break down**, do they:

a stop for a short time because both sides want a rest?
b end because both sides have reached an agreement?
c end because the two sides cannot agree?

GRAMMAR

Which of these are grammatically possible?

a We broke down the talks.
b The talks broke down.
c The talks were broken down.
d The talks broke themselves down.
e The talks are breaking down.

→ Now check your answers in the key.

Practise

1 Choose the best word to complete each of these sentences:

a The *conversations/debates/talks* with the unions broke down over pay.
b The *appointment/deal/meeting* has broken down because the shareholders want more money.
c If these *contracts/negotiations/speeches* break down, there will be a trade war.

2 Complete these sentences using an appropriate form of **break down**:

a The deal _____ as neither side was prepared to compromise.

b If these talks _____ , there could be a strike.

c Discussions between the two sides _____ when they started discussing pay.

d Talks with foreign investors are in danger of _____

e When the deal _____ each side blamed the other.

f The friendly relationship between the two companies has _____ over the question of copyright.

→ Now check your answers in the key.

Build your vocabulary

RELATED WORDS   NOUN: **a breakdown** (This noun is usually singular)
▶ *Who was responsible for the **breakdown** of the talks?*
▶ *There has been a **breakdown** in the relationship between the two companies.*

9 break something down (into something)

Study Read these sentences carefully.

- ▶ I have **broken** the sales figures **down** into regions.
- ▶ The software **breaks down** the results by time and frequency.
- ▶ The job's easier if you **break** it **down** into smaller tasks.
- ▶ The data **was broken down** into six different categories.

Check

Use the sentences in the Study box to help you do these exercises.

MEANING

If you **break something down**, do you:

a reduce its price so that it is very cheap?

b destroy it by cutting it into small pieces?

c divide it into smaller pieces so that it is easier to do or understand?

GRAMMAR

Which of these are grammatically possible?

a I will break down the sales results.
b I will break them down.
c I will break down them.
d The sales results broke down.
e The sales results were broken down.

→ Now check your answers in the key.

Practise

1 Match the two halves to make complete sentences

a The economy can be broken down into
b The structure of the company is broken down into
c If you break production costs down in
d He broke the project down into
e Let's break the PA's duties down into

i 6 different departments.
ii separate tasks to see how busy she is.
iii the report, we can see the problem.
iv sectors according to the type of industry.
v several stages.

2 Read the text and find and underline *two* verbs that could be replaced by a form of **break down**. Then correct and rewrite the sentences below the text using a form of **break down**.

> Henry Ford's most famous car was the Model T. In order to make this car, he invented a new system of production: the assembly line. On Ford's assembly line, the manufacture of a car was divided into 84 simple tasks each done by a different worker. By separating out production in this way, he was able to speed up production and reduce labour costs. In the process, he started a revolution in manufacturing.

a On an assembly line, production is divided into a few complex tasks.

_____

b Ford separated the production of the Model T into 54 tasks.

_____

→ Now check your answers in the key.

Build your vocabulary

RELATED WORDS   NOUN: **a breakdown** (= division of something larger into smaller parts.) (This noun is usually singular)
   ▶ *Can you give me a **breakdown** of the sales figures by Monday?*

10 break into something

Study Read these sentences carefully.

▸ The company has not yet managed to **break into** the software market.
▸ It is hard for new companies to **break into** the industry.
▸ She is well aware that **breaking into** journalism will not be easy.
▸ The US market is huge and we need to **break into** it.

Check

Use the sentences in the Study box to help you do these exercises.

MEANING

1 Complete the meaning of **break into something** by using the words below:

industry   successful   involved

to start to become _____ in a particular activity or _____
that is difficult to get into and to become _____ at it

2 Which of the following can you **break into**?

a market   an industry   a contract   a job   a new office   a career

GRAMMAR

Which of these are grammatically correct?

a They have broken into the US market.
b They have broken into it.
c They have broken into.
d The US market has been broken into.

→ Now check your answers in the key.

Practise

1 There is **one** error in each of the following sentences. Find it and correct it.

a The firm is expanding and has already broke into the European market.
b So far she has failed to break in the music business.
c Two years ago we broke the mass market with a range of low-priced electronic goods.

2 Complete these sentences using a form of **break into** and one of the phrases below:

the restaurant business   the toy industry   the budget travel market   the top ten companies

a The airline faces a tough task to _____ .

b He had spent years as a chef but still couldn't _____ .

c They had been number 12 for years, but finally they _____
_____ .

d Now she's very successful, but ten years ago she hadn't even _____
_____ .

→ Now check your answers in the key.

11 break something up; break itself up

Study Read these sentences carefully.

▶ The new owners decided to **break up** the company **into** several separate groups.
▶ They have **broken up** the business to pay off some of the debt.
▶ We don't buy companies just to **break** them **up**.
▶ The business may have to be **broken up** and sold in parts.
▶ The insurer will sell its assets or **break** itself **up**.

Check

Use the sentences in the Study box to help you do these exercises.

MEANING

Which of the following means the same as to **break up** a company?

a to divide a company into smaller parts
b to make a company no longer exist

GRAMMAR

Two of these sentences have a grammatical mistake. Find them and correct them.

a They broke the company up.
b The company was forced to break up itself.
c They broke up the company.
d The company was broken.

→ Now check your answers in the key.

Practise

1 Rewrite the following sentences so that the meaning stays the same, using a form of **break something up** and any other words that you need.

a It was decided to split the publishing department into four separate divisions.
It was decided _____

b Businesses are often divided into smaller units as they grow larger.
Businesses _____

c The company is now two separate businesses.
The company has _____

2 Answer these questions in a suitable way, including a form of **break up** in each answer.

a Does the company still exist?
Yes, but _____

b Is the new managing director going to change anything about the company?
Yes, _____

→ Now check your answers in the key.

Build your vocabulary

RELATED WORDS **To break up** can also be used without an object, meaning 'to be divided into smaller parts'.

▶ *As companies get larger, they may **break up** into smaller units.*

NOUN: **break-up** This is a countable noun.

▶ *He tried to prevent the **break-up** of his group.*

12 bring something forward

▸ We might have to **bring** the meeting **forward** to tomorrow.
▸ The company is likely to **bring forward** the opening date of their new plant.
▸ If you cannot attend an interview on May 7th, we can **bring** it **forward** by a week.
▸ The new car is ready so the launch can be **brought forward**.

Check

Use the sentences in the Study box to help you do these exercises.

MEANING

Which of the following is the best explanation of the meaning of **bring something forward**?

a to make something happen at a later time than planned
b to make something happen at an earlier time than planned

GRAMMAR

One of these sentences is grammatically incorrect. Find and correct the mistake.

a They brought the meeting forward.
b They brought it forward.
c They brought forward the meeting.
d The meeting brought forward.

→ Now check your answers in the key.

Practise

Reply to the following statements using the verb **bring forward**, one of the phrases below and any other words that you need.

| by two weeks | to Monday | to 2 o'clock | to March 17th |

a I thought the meeting was on Wednesday, not Monday.
   It was first planned for Wednesday, but _____

b We're supposed to be having a training session at 4 o'clock but the training room is being used.
   Can't we _____

c I'd prefer to have the interview before I go on holiday next month.
   Why don't you see if you can _____?

d I thought they had arranged the sales conference for March 24th.
   They have now _____

→ Now check your answers in the key.

Build your vocabulary

SYNONYMS **put something forward**:
   ▸ We've **put** the meeting **forward** to 12.30.

OPPOSITES **Put something back** can be used as the opposite of this meaning of **bring something forward**.
   ▸ *The opening of the new factory has been **put back** three weeks.*

   Postpone something can also be used:
   ▸ *The meeting has been **postponed** until next week.*

13 bring somebody in

Study Read these sentences carefully.

- We're planning to **bring in** a new team of managers.
- Some companies do not like **bringing** experts **in** from outside.
- She has run a similar project, so the CEO has **brought** her **in** on this one.
- Financial consultants were **brought in** to assess the business.

Check

Use the sentences in the Study box to help you do these exercises.

MEANING

Choose the best meaning for
bring somebody in.

a to ask somebody to leave a project
b to invite somebody to give a speech
c to get somebody involved in
   something to help or advise

GRAMMAR

Which of these are grammatically possible?

a We're bringing in a team of experts.
b We're bringing a team of experts in.
c We're bringing in them to help.
d We're bringing them in to help.
e A team of experts was brought in.

→ Now check your answers in the key.

Practise

1 Answer the following questions, using an appropriate form of **bring in**
and one of the following words and phrases:

> a new managing director   a partner   a lawyer
> a financial adviser   an architect   a team of experts

a How can we decide where to invest the company's money?
  We could _____

b How was the problem solved?
  A _____

c What is the next step in our plans for new offices?
  It's time to _____

d I think there is a problem with this contract.
  We should have _____

e How did they get the company out of its difficulties?
  I heard they had _____ *to run it.*

f How does she cope with all the clients she's got now?
  I think she's planning _____

2 Read the following piece from a newspaper and then write a suitable headline
using a form of **bring in**.

> A local catering firm had a team of famous chefs to help them prepare a dinner to raise money
> for children's charities. The event was held on March 12 in the Town Hall and raised over £6 000.

_____

→ Now check your answers in the key.

14 bring something in; bring something into something

- The deals will **bring in** more than $5 million.
- The business **brought in** a good profit.
- The event should have **brought** more money **in** from shoppers than it did.
- They hope the price changes will **bring** more cash **into** the business.

Check

Use the sentences in the Study box to help you do these exercises.

MEANING

Which of the following is closest in meaning to **bring something in**?

a to earn an amount of money
b to cost a particular amount of money
c to spend an amount of money

GRAMMAR

There is a mistake in **one** of these sentences. Find it and correct it.

a The deal brought in $5 billion.
b The deal brought it in $5 billion.
c The deal brought $5 billion in.
d The deals brought more money in.

→ Now check your answers in the key.

Practise

1 Match the two halves together to make complete sentences.

a She hopes to bring in extra
b The museum brings in about
c The IT system brings in billions
d The industry has brought in foreign investment

i $150 000 from tourists.
ii revenue by offering delivery services.
iii worth $15 billion to Africa.
iv in profits.

2 Complete the sentences with an appropriate form of **bring in**.

a The sale might _____ €1 million if we are lucky.

b He has _____ 80% of the company's sales.

c The changes should _____ much-needed cash.

d The group _____ revenues of ¥105 billion last year.

e Our division usually _____ 35% of total revenue.

→ Now check your answers in the key.

Build your vocabulary

OTHER MEANINGS If a person **brings in** money, they earn it, for example from their job:

- *How much is she **bringing in** every month?*
- *His job only **brought** him **in** a small income.*

Bring somebody or **something in** can also mean 'to attract somebody or something to a place or business':

- *We changed the store's hours to **bring in** more customers.*
- *They were under pressure to **bring in** business.*
- *The new lower prices are **bringing** shoppers **into** the store.*

15 bring something out

- The company **brought out** a range of luxury cosmetics last spring.
- They seem to **bring** a new product **out** every month.
- Drug companies have to test all new drugs before **bringing** them **out**.
- The book will be **brought out** early next year.

Check

Use the sentences in the Study box to help you do these exercises.

MEANING

Which of the following means the same as **bring something out**?

a to stop selling a product
b to copy and sell an existing product
c to produce and sell a new product

GRAMMAR

Which of these are grammatically possible?

a They brought out a new product last month.
b They brought it out last month.
c They brought out it last month.
d It was brought out last month.

→ Now check your answers in the key.

Practise

1 There is <u>one</u> mistake in each of these sentences. Find it and correct it.

a Many fast-food chains now bringing out new ranges of healthier foods.
b The car was extremely popular when Fiat first brought it.

2 Complete the following sentences with the correct form of **bring out** and one of the words below:

> model   it   version   titles   editions

a The auto manufacturer _____ a new _____ of the car last year.

b Magazine publishers are _____ a range of _____ that target male consumers.

c They will probably _____ an up-dated _____ of the software sometime next year.

d The _____ was not very successful when the company first _____ it _____ .

→ Now check your answers in the key.

Build your vocabulary

SIMILAR VERBS **Come out with something** can be used instead of **bring something out**.
  - *The company has **come out with** a new version of the software.*

  Come out is often used instead of **be brought out**:
  - *Her new book **is coming out** in the new year.*

16 bring something up

Study Read these sentences carefully.
- ▶ She didn't **bring up** the subject of money immediately.
- ▶ Every time I **bring** the matter **up**, he changes the subject.
- ▶ I'm going to **bring** it **up** with my manager at our next meeting.
- ▶ Some interesting questions were **brought up** at the conference.

Check

Use the sentences in the Study box to help you do these exercises.

MEANING

What is the best explanation of this meaning of **bring something up**?

a to start talking about something
b to invent something
c to lift something

GRAMMAR

Which of these are grammatically possible?

a He brought it up at the meeting.
b He brought the subject up at the meeting.
c He brought up it at the meeting.
d The subject wasn't brought up at the meeting.

→ Now check your answers in the key.

Practise

Complete the following sentences using a form of **bring something up** in each and a pronoun **(it)** where necessary.

a I think we all need to discuss this.

  OK. Can you _____ at the next meeting?

b I don't think I'll finish the work by the deadline.

  You'd better _____ with your manager.

c Have you discussed money with them?

  No. I haven't _____ yet.

d I'm not happy with our current supplier.

  Why didn't you _____ earlier?

e Did she mention overtime pay at the meeting?

  That was the first topic that _____

→ Now check your answers in the key.

Build your vocabulary

SYNONYMS   **Raise something** means the same but is more formal:
  ▶ *Anna **raised** this subject at the meeting.*

SIMILAR VERBS   **Come up** means 'to appear' or 'to be mentioned' and does not have an object. It is used with similar words to *bring something up*, for example an **issue**, a **point**, **matter** or **subject** can *come up*:
  ▶ *This issue **came up** at our last meeting.*

17 build something up

Study Read these sentences carefully.

- ▸ A salesman must first **build up** a network of contacts.
- ▸ I **built** the company **up** from nothing.
- ▸ She started the business in 1999 and has **built** it **up** gradually.
- ▸ The company's reputation has been **built up** over many years.

Check

Use the sentences in the Study box to help you do these exercises.

MEANING

Which of these verbs is closest in meaning to this meaning of **build something up**?

a to increase
b to get
c to develop
d to improve

GRAMMAR

Which of these are grammatically possible?

a He built the business up.
b He built up the business.
c He built it up.
d He built up it.
e The business was built up by my father.

→ Now check your answers in the key.

Practise

1 Complete the following sentences with an appropriate form of **build up** and one of the objects below:

new collections   a picture   a good relationship   a large group of clients

a It's important _____ with your customers.

b He has spent the last 10 years _____

c Each year fashion houses have to _____

d From our market research we have _____ of what customers want.

2 Rewrite the following sentences so that the meaning stays the same, using a form of **build up** and any other words you need.

a They gradually built the company up over 20 years.

The company _____

b Some firms never manage to develop a strong management team.

Not all firms _____

c If you want to be successful you must collect good contacts.

He said that if I _____

d She quickly developed a reputation as an honest and reliable worker.

It didn't take her long _____

→ Now check your answers in the key.

18 burn out; burn yourself out

Study Read these sentences carefully.
- ▶ It's a high-pressure job and many people **burn out** and leave.
- ▶ As we neared the launch date, people were **burning out**.
- ▶ If he carries on working so hard, he'll **burn** himself **out**.
- ▶ By the age of 30, many commodity traders have **burnt** themselves **out**.

Check

Use the sentences in the Study box to help you do these exercises.

MEANING

If you **burn out** or **burn yourself out**, do you:

a spend all your money?
b work on a project for another company?
c work much too hard?

GRAMMAR

Which of these are grammatically possible?
a He burnt out.
b He burnt himself out.
c He burnt out himself.
d He was burnt out by his employer.

→ Now check your answers in the key.

Practise

1 Complete the following sentences using a form of **burn out** or **burn yourself out** and any other words you need.

a If you make your staff work too many extra hours a week, they might

_____ .

b Because they work at such a fast pace, people in the City often

_____ a young age.

c You can't keep up that level of work without _____ .

d TV producers work very long hours. I've seen quite a few who _____ .

e She never took a break from work and eventually _____ .

2 Answer the following questions:

a Do you know anyone who burnt themselves out by working too hard?

_____

b Can you think of any professions where it is common for people to burn out?

_____

c What are some ways of avoiding burning yourself out?

_____

→ Now check your answers in the key.

Build your vocabulary

RELATED WORDS   NOUN: **burnout.** (This is usually used as an uncountable noun.)
*You risk **burnout** if you work such long hours.*

ADJECTIVE: **burnt out** or **burned out**
- ▶ *It was a high-pressure job that left him **burnt out** and exhausted.*
- ▶ *a **burned-out** executive*

19 buy somebody or something out

Study Read these sentences carefully.

- He **bought out** his partners and expanded the company.
- Two French businessmen tried to **buy** the firm **out**.
- I don't have enough money to **buy** her **out**.
- The company was **bought out** by its management.

Check

Use the sentences in the Study box to help you do these exercises.

MEANING

Choose the best explanation of this meaning of **buy somebody or something out**:

a to buy as much of something as possible
b to buy part or all of a business from somebody else

GRAMMAR

Which of these are grammatically possible?

a They bought the company out.
b He was bought out by his partner.
c His partner bought him out.
d They bought out it.
e They bought it out in 2004.

→ Now check your answers in the key.

Practise

1 Rearrange the words to make complete sentences:

a to want I partner buy my out
b been by of group a company has its out the employees bought

2 Complete the sentences using an appropriate form of **buy out**.

a She had _____ her partner.

b The telecom company has agreed a deal to _____
   the two main shareholders.

c He hopes that a big firm will _____ him _____
   and he can retire a millionaire.

3 Rewrite the following sentences so that the meaning stays the same, using the correct form of **buy out**.

a If you want to have complete control of the business, why don't you buy her share?
   If _____

b The fund has bought the shares of other investors at $101.50 a share.

   _____

→ Now check your answers in the key.

Build your vocabulary

RELATED WORDS NOUN: **buyout** This is a countable noun.
- *The management are considering a **buyout** of the company* (= they want to buy enough shares so that they gain control of it).

20 call back

Study Read these sentences carefully.

▸ Can you photocopy these documents for me? I'll **call back** later to collect them.
▸ I'm afraid no one can see you at the moment. Can you **call back** in half an hour?
▸ The sales rep **called back** the following week with some samples.

Check

Use the sentences in the Study box to help you do these exercises.

MEANING

If you **call back**, what do you do? Choose the correct words.

You go to **a different/the same** place to see somebody **again/for the first time**.

GRAMMAR

Which of these are grammatically possible?

a I called back later.
b I called it back later.
c I called back the office later.
d I called back at the office later.

→ Now check your answers in the key.

Practise

1 Match up the two halves of the dialogues :

a 'Can I see Ms Johnson please?'
b 'I called back but you weren't there.'
c 'He's called back several times. I think you'd better see him.'

i 'Yes, I'm sorry. I was in a meeting.'
ii 'OK. Show him in.'
iii 'I'm afraid she's out, can you call back later?'

2 Write an appropriate sentence using **call back**:

a Somebody comes to your office and asks for your colleague. She is at lunch at the moment. Ask them to come back after lunch.

_____

b You deliver some documents but forget to bring one of them. Say you will return tomorrow with the other document.

_____

c You sell somebody a photocopier. Tell them you will come back in 3 months to check the machine.

_____

→ Now check your answers in the key.

Build your vocabulary

SIMILAR VERBS When somebody goes to visit a person to sell something or provide a service, they **call on** them. When they visit for a second time, they **call back**, or **call again**:

▸ I'll **call again** next week to finalize the arrangements.

When somebody **calls back**, they make a **follow-up call** or a **follow-up visit**:

▸ It's best to make a **follow-up call** within a few days to confirm the sale.

21 carry something out

- We need to **carry out** an assessment of the risks.
- When do they think they'll be able to **carry** the repairs **out**?
- These changes are so expensive that very few companies can **carry** them **out**.
- Safety checks were **carried out** by inspectors.

Check

Use the sentences in the Study box to help you do these exercises.

MEANING

Which of the following words could you use instead of **carry out** in the sentence below?

taking   playing   doing   passing

*Scientists are currently **carrying out** tests to discover the cause of the problem.*

GRAMMAR

Which of these are grammatically possible?

a The research was carried out by an analyst.

b An analyst carried out the research.

c It was an analyst who carried it out.

d It was an analyst who carried out it.

→ Now check your answers in the key.

Practise

1 Complete these sentences using the correct form of **carry out**.

a We _____ safety checks every two weeks.

b The two audits were _____ by D&T.

c My job is to _____ a review of procedures.

d A third of US government bond trades are now _____ electronically.

2 Write sentences using one of the nouns below and a different form of **carry out** in each. One is done for you as an example.

tests   investigation   work   research   inspection

a *An investigation is being carried out by the company's auditors.*

b _____

c _____

d _____

e _____

→ Now check your answers in the key.

Build your vocabulary

OTHER MEANINGS **Carry something out** can also mean 'to do something that you have promised to do or that someone has asked you to do':
- *He **carried out** his threat to sue the company.*
- *You didn't **carry out** my instructions correctly.*

22 cash in (on something)

Check

Use the sentences in the Study box to help you do these exercises.

MEANING

If you **cash in on something**, what do you do? Choose the best meaning.

a you spend a lot of money on something
b you earn a lot of money by working very hard at something
c you earn a lot of money by taking advantage of a situation

GRAMMAR

Which of these are grammatically possible?

a He cashed in.
b He cashed in the situation.
c He cashed the situation in.
d He cashed in on the situation.
e The situation was cashed in.

→ Now check your answers in the key.

Practise

1 Match the halves to make complete sentences:

a Shoppers often go across the border to
b The singer was keen to
c The company is now
d She made a fortune when she

i cashing in on the rise in steel prices.
ii cash in on the favourable exchange rate.
iii cashed in on the IT boom of the 1990s.
iv cash in on her recent publicity.

2 Rewrite the following sentences replacing the words in *italic* with a form of **cash in (on)**.

a The banks have *taken advantage of* the growing demand for credit.

_____

b There is a huge market for these products and many companies have been *making big profits*.

_____

c Reality TV shows are very popular and several TV companies are trying to *make money from* them.

_____

→ Now check your answers in the key.

Build your vocabulary

SIMILAR VERBS   To **profit from something** is more formal:
- *She shouldn't be **profiting from** her crime.*

OTHER MEANINGS   To **cash something in** means 'to exchange something for money':
- *You will lose money if you **cash** your policy **in** early.*

23 catch on

Study Read these sentences carefully.
- Shopping on the Internet has really **caught on** now.
- Many new inventions take a long time to **catch on** with the public.
- The compact car is rapidly **catching on** among Chinese consumers.
- The brand has been slow to **catch on** in Europe.

Check

Use the sentences in the Study box to help you do these exercises.

MEANING

Which of the following best describes this meaning of **catch on**?

a to reach the same level or standard
b to become fashionable or popular

GRAMMAR

Which of these are grammatically possible?

a The idea never caught on.
b The idea never caught on with the public.
c The idea was never caught on.
d The idea will never catch on.

→ Now check your answers in the key.

Practise

1 Rewrite the following sentences so that the meaning stays the same, using one of the forms of **catch on** below and any other words you need.

| has caught on | wouldn't catch on | haven't caught on | is catching on | have caught on |

a More and more people are using broadband.

Broadband _____

b Older people aren't interested in buying camera phones.

Camera phones _____

c Many people now send electronic greetings cards.

Electronic greetings cards _____

d Forty years ago, people thought that no one in the UK would buy duvets.

Forty years ago, people thought that _____

2 Using a form of the verb **catch on** write **four** sentences, two about things that have or might become popular or fashionable and two about things that have failed to become popular or fashionable. Here are some ideas to get you started: **cellphones, jogging, Concorde, video phones**…

_____

_____

_____

_____

→ Now check your answers in the key.

24 clean something up

Check

Use the sentences in the Study box to help you do these exercises.

MEANING

Complete the explanation of this meaning of **clean something up** with words from the brackets.

to (**change/improve**) something such as an organization or a system by (**removing/adding**) parts or people that are (**dishonest/old-fashioned**)

GRAMMAR

Which of these are grammatically possible?

a They have cleaned up the industry.
b They have cleaned the industry up.
c They have cleaned up it.
d They have cleaned it up.
e The industry has been cleaned up.

→ Now check your answers in the key.

Practise

Complete these sentences with an appropriate form of **clean up** and a pronoun where necessary.

a She is _____ the image of the department.

b These measures are aimed at _____ the banking sector.

c The industry does not operate to high enough standards, and we intend to

_____ .

d If the company _____ its image, it may attract new customers.

e The new governor has promised that the political system will _____ .

→ Now check your answers in the key.

Build your vocabulary

RELATED WORDS   NOUN: **a clean-up** (This is usually used in the singular.)
▸ *The government has promised a **clean-up** of the insurance and pensions industry.*

IDIOMS   **To clean up your act** means 'to start behaving in a more moral or responsible way':
▸ *She believes that the financial services industry needs to **clean up its act**.*

OTHER MEANINGS   **Clean something up** can also mean 'to make an organization financially stronger or reduce the amount of debt it has':
▸ *We are **cleaning up** our finances by cutting spending.*
▸ *The bank's bad loans need to be **cleaned up**.*

25 close something down; close down

- The company has **closed down** its loss-making stores.
- They made a mistake in **closing** the business **down**.
- They opened a branch in Tokyo 10 years ago, but they recently **closed** it **down**.
- The factory was **closed down**, with the loss of 750 jobs.
- Many smaller stores have **closed down** due to a lack of business.

Check

Use the sentences in the Study box to help you do these exercises.

MEANING

If somebody **closes down** a factory, business, etc. which **one** of the following is true?

a They close it for the night.
b They close it permanently.
c They reduce the number of workers.

GRAMMAR

Which of these are grammatically possible?

a The factory closed down.
b The factory was closed down.
c He closed the factory down.
d He closed down it.

→ Now check your answers in the key.

Practise

1 Choose the correct form of **close down** for each sentence and write it in the space:

a The store is going _____ because of poor sales.
   closing down/to close down/closed down

b The mine was _____ in 1997.
   closing down/closed down/close down

c The business is losing money and managers may be forced to _____ .
   close down/close it down/close down it

2 Answer these questions using a form of **close down** and any other words you need:

a How are they going to cut costs?
   They are planning _____ *their South African office.*

b Why did they lose their jobs?
   Because their factory _____

c What happened when the store started to lose money?
   The managers decided _____

→ Now check your answers in the key.

Build your vocabulary

RELATED WORDS NOUN: **a close-down** (This is uncountable or singular.)
- *They have announced the **close-down** of their UK operations.*

SYNONYMS **Shut something down, shut down**
- *They **shut** the factory **down** last year.*

OPPOSITES → **open up, open something up** on page 59

26 contract something out (to somebody)

Study Read these sentences carefully.
- ▸ We **contract out** most of our IT work.
- ▸ The company **contracts** the printing **out** to a private firm.
- ▸ They have stopped doing their own catering and now **contract** it **out**.
- ▸ Training is often **contracted out** to specialist firms.

Check

Use the sentences in the Study box to help you do these exercises.

MEANING

Choose the best words to complete this meaning of **contract something out**.

to **arrange/wait** for **work/tests** to be done by **your own/another** company rather than by **your own/another**

GRAMMAR

Which of these are grammatically possible?

a They contract out the cleaning.
b They contract the cleaning out.

c They contract out.
d The cleaning is contracted out.

→ Now check your answers in the key.

Practise

1 Read the text below and then answer the questions.

> The A&B publishing company has decided to contract out its UK transportation to Taylor Trucks. The decision was made because the company's own transport department could no longer deal with increased demand. The company has been contracting out its transportation abroad for the past three years and has reduced its costs significantly.

a Who will be paid to transport goods in the UK for A&B?

_____

b Does A&B transport its own goods abroad?

_____

c What is the result of this?

_____

2 Rewrite the sentences using a form of **contract out**, the words in brackets (…) and any other words you need.

a The company does not do its own advertising.

The company _____ *(its advertising)*

b We pay another company to do our office cleaning.

We _____ *(the office cleaning)*

→ Now check your answers in the key.

Build your vocabulary

SYNONYMS   To **outsource** something:
> ▸ *Many companies **outsource** design and advertising.*

27 copy somebody **in** (**on** something)

Study Read these sentences carefully.

▸ The program allows you to **copy** any number of people **in on** emails.
▸ I'll send a memo to the personnel department and **copy** you **in**.
▸ I would like to be **copied in on** all correspondence.
▸ That's an important email – it's worth **copying** everyone **in**.

Check

Use the sentences in the Study box to help you do these exercises.

MEANING

If you **copy somebody in** do you:

a write something in exactly the same way as somebody else?
b send somebody a copy of an email, a letter, etc.?

GRAMMAR

Which of these are grammatically possible?

a I'll copy you in.
b I'll copy in you.
c I'll copy John in on the email.
d I was copied in on most of the emails.

→ Now check your answers in the key.

Practise

1 Put the words in the correct order to make a sentence.

a you me in copy on the can email?
b him copy on I my all in correspondence.
c important is her all copy it to in on emails.

2 Rewrite the parts of the following sentences in brackets so that the meaning stays the same, using an appropriate form of **copy in** and any other words you need.

a Would you like me to (send you a copy) when I write back to her?

_____

b It is essential to (send a copy of all correspondence to your secretary).

_____

c Why didn't you (send me a copy of your report)?

_____

→ Now check your answers in the key.

Build your vocabulary

RELATED WORDS When you **copy somebody in** on an email, etc., you write **cc** and the person's name so that other people know who has received a copy:

▸ *MEMO: To Jan West, Sales Department.* **cc** *Mark Bates, Personnel Department*

SIMILAR VERBS You can also use **copy something to somebody**, especially for a letter:

▸ *I have **copied** the letter **to** our legal experts.*

In American English, **copy somebody** can be used with this meaning:

▸ *All senior managers should have been **copied**.*

28 cut back (on something); cut something back

- ▸ The company will need to **cut back** if it wants to meet its spending targets.
- ▸ A lot of businesses have **cut back on** managerial staff.
- ▸ During the recession, many companies **cut back** technology spending.
- ▸ The company has **cut** output **back** by 2%.
- ▸ Our expenses are far too high – we'll have to **cut** them **back**.
- ▸ Production has been **cut back** dramatically.

Check

Use the sentences in the Study box to help you do these exercises.

MEANING

Delete the **one** choice which is not appropriate.

If a company or an organization **cuts back**, it reduces…

a the amount of money it spends
b the number of people it employs
c the amount of something it produces
d the amount of profit it makes

GRAMMAR

Which of these are grammatically possible?

a We have cut back spending.
b We have cut spending back.
c We have cut it back on.
d We have cut it back.
e Spending has been cut back.

→ Now check your answers in the key.

Practise

1 Delete the **one** unnecessary word from each of the following sentences.

a A lot of firms had to cut back on during the recession.
b Expenditure on essential services will not be cut it back .
c Consumers cut back on it their borrowing in November.

2 Rewrite the following sentences so that the meaning stays the same, using an appropriate form of **cut back** or **cut back on** and any other words you need.

a In order to reduce inflation, the government must spend less.

In order to reduce inflation, the government must _____ *spending.*

b The amount that the firm produces will be reduced in the next few years.

The firm's production _____

c To cut costs, we reduced the number of people we employ.

To cut costs, we _____ *staff.*

d The amount of money given to this project has been dramatically reduced.

The funding for _____

→ Now check your answers in the key.

Build your vocabulary

RELATED WORDS NOUN: **cutback** (This is usually used in the plural.)
- ▸ *There have been **cutbacks** in spending over the last three years.*

29 deal with something

- ▸ Staff should know how to **deal with** an emergency.
- ▸ I've got far too much paperwork to **deal with**!
- ▸ What you have to do is face the situation and **deal with** it.
- ▸ Customer complaints should be **dealt with** quickly.

Check

Use the sentences in the Study box to help you do these exercises.

MEANING

Choose the best explanation for this meaning of **deal with something**.

a to arrange a business deal
b to sell something
c to solve a problem or perform a task

GRAMMAR

Which of these are grammatically possible?

a She dealt with the problem.
b She dealt it with.
c She dealt with it.
d The problem was dealt with.

→ Now check your answers in the key.

Practise

1 Complete the sentences with an appropriate form of **deal with**.

a If something's not going well, tell us so that we can _____ it.

b Banks are _____ bad loans aggressively now.

c There are many important subjects for the new board to _____ .

d We have _____ all the challenges we faced.

2 Complete the sentences by using the correct form of **deal with** and one of the three possible **nouns** or **pronouns**.

a We need to _____ the *tables/situation/conference* before it gets worse.

b The *matter/computer/office* will be _____ by senior managers.

c My job involves _____ *lights/complaints/advice* from customers.

d He told me about the problem and asked me to _____ *him/it/them*.

3 Write one or two sentence describing problems or challenges that you face in your job, using a form of **deal with** in each one.

_____

_____

→ Now check your answers in the key.

Build your vocabulary

OTHER MEANINGS   **To deal with something or somebody** can also mean 'to do business with a person, a company or an organization':
> ▸ We have **dealt with** the company for many years without a problem.

To deal with somebody can mean 'to look after or talk to somebody in an appropriate way' and is used especially about things you do in your job:
> ▸ Her job involves **dealing with** customers on the phone.

30 dispose of something

Study Read these sentences carefully.

▸ The company had to **dispose of** some of its assets to raise money.
▸ The IT company **disposed of** its hardware division for $10.4 million.
▸ The shares were no longer a good investment, and we felt it was time to **dispose of** them.
▸ The remaining land was **disposed of** for development.

Check

Use the sentences in the Study box to help you do these exercises.

MEANING

Use the words below to complete the meaning of **dispose of**.

asset   shares   sell

to _____ an

_____

such as land, property, or

_____

GRAMMAR

Which of these are grammatically possible?

a They disposed of their assets.
b They disposed their assets of.
c They disposed of them.
d Their assets were disposed of.

→ Now check your answers in the key.

Practise

1 Replace the <u>underlined</u> verbs in the following sentences with an appropriate form of **dispose of**.

a He **sold** 20 000 shares on Wednesday.
b The university did not need those buildings and so **got rid of** them.
c The shipping group was set to **sell off** its 50% stake in the cruise company.
d The business raised money by **selling off** some property it owned.

2 Complete the following text by adding an appropriate form of **dispose of** in each gap.

(a) _____ assets is often a quick and easy way for a business to raise capital for investments, but choosing which assets to (b) _____ can be difficult. Stocks and shares can be (c) _____ easily, but it can take more time to (d) _____ land or property. However, businesses do need assets, and these can be difficult to replace once they have been (e) _____ .

→ Now check your answers in the key.

Build your vocabulary

RELATED WORDS   NOUN: **disposal** (This can be countable and uncountable.)
▸ *They raised money through the **disposal** of some assets.*

OTHER MEANINGS   **Dispose of** also has a more general meaning – 'to get rid of something that you do not want or need':
▸ *Businesses must **dispose of** toxic waste carefully and safely.*

31 draw something up

Study Read these sentences carefully.
- Managers are **drawing up** guidelines on safety at work.
- I **drew up** a list of 10 products that I could sell online.
- We needed a business plan and I was asked to **draw** it **up**.
- A new contract was **drawn up**.

Check

Use the sentences in the Study box to help you do these exercises.

MEANING

Choose the best words to complete the meaning of **draw something up**:

to prepare and (*argue/paint/write*) something such as a (*debate/document/picture*) or plan

GRAMMAR

Which of these are grammatically correct?

a I drew up the document.
b I drew up it.
c I drew the document up.

d The document was drawn up.
e I drew it up.

→ Now check your answers in the key.

Practise

1 Complete the sentences below, using the correct form of **draw up** and the most suitable noun from the choices underneath each sentence.

a You should ask a lawyer to _____ the _____ for you.
   picture/process/document

b She is busy _____ a _____ for the new employees.
   map/contract/business

c The committee has _____ some new _____
   rules/members/CDs

d I'll _____ a _____ of people to invite.
   table/session/list

2 Rewrite the following sentences so the meaning stays the same, using **draw something up**.

a We're writing some new guidelines.

_____

b I need to write a report for my boss.

_____

c The contract was produced last year.

_____

d The company is working on plans for a new project.

_____

→ Now check your answers in the key.

32 drop off

Check

Use the sentences in the Study box to help you do these exercises.

MEANING

Which one of these verbs means the same as **drop off**?

a to increase
b to stay the same
c to decrease

GRAMMAR

Which of these are grammatically possible?

a Sales have dropped off.
b Sales have dropped it off.
c Sales were dropped off.
d Sales are dropping off.

→ Now check your answers in the key.

Practise

1 Replace one verb in each of the following sentences with a suitable form of **drop off**, without changing the meaning.

a Profits have been steady but are expected to fall in the next six months.

_____

b Demand for the product has decreased although the supply has improved.

_____

c Sales usually increase around January and decrease in the summer months.

_____

d We expect our profits to be lower as income from advertising has fallen.

_____

2 Complete the sentences using an appropriate form of **drop off** and one of the adverbs:

sharply   dramatically   noticeably

a The number of customers has _____ .
b Auto sales continued to _____ in the winter.
c Results were lower than expected after foreign business _____ .

→ Now check your answers in the key.

Build your vocabulary

RELATED WORDS   NOUN: **drop-off.** (This is used as a singular noun)
▸ *The industry has seen a sharp* **drop-off** *in business.*

SYNONYMS   **To fall off** has the same meaning and is used in the same way:
▸ *Demand for the product has* **fallen off**.

There is also a noun **fall-off**, used in the singular.

33 drum up something

Check

Use the sentences in the Study box to help you do these exercises.

MEANING

1 Which of the following best describes the meaning of **drum up** something?

  a to work hard to get something
  b to make a lot of noise about something

2 Which one of the following is **not** a way of **drumming up** business?

  a offering discounts
  b calling on potential customers
  c raising prices
  d giving away free gifts with a product

GRAMMAR

Which of these are grammatically possible?

  a They drummed up more business.
  b They drummed up it.
  c They drummed it up.
  d More business was drummed up.

→ Now check your answers in the key.

Practise

1 Complete the sentences using an appropriate form of **drum up** and one of the words or phrases below:

new business   customers   cash   more visitors   interest

  a The job of the sales force is to go round calling on potential customers and _____ .

  b They need to _____ to pay off some of their debt.

  c They are planning a huge TV advertising campaign to _____ in the new brand.

  d There are some great deals at the moment as lenders try new ways of _____ .

  e The lower entry price has _____ for the museum.

2 You are starting a new business from home. Suggest some ways of **drumming up** business.

_____
_____
_____

→ Now check your answers in the key.

34 dry up

Study Read these sentences carefully.
- ▸ Costs are rising and income is **drying up**.
- ▸ She is worried about what will happen if her work **dries up**.
- ▸ We are cutting back production as orders have almost **dried up**.

Check

Use the sentences in the Study box to help you do these exercises.

MEANING

Choose the best words to complete the meaning of this use of **dry up**:

if a *part/supply* of something **dries up**, there is *suddenly/gradually less/more* of it until there is *some/none* left.

GRAMMAR

Which one of these is grammatically possible?

a The money dried up.
b The money dried itself up.
c The money was dried up.

→ Now check your answers in the key.

Practise

1 Rewrite the sentences below using a form of **dry up** in your answer.

a There is no more work at all.

Work _____

b Orders from abroad could stop at any time.

Orders _____

c There is much less demand for our products now.

Demand _____

2 The graph below shows the level of a company's sales between 1997 and 2005. Write two sentences describing how sales changed during this period, using a form of **dry up** in each. Here are some other words you can use: **orders, customers, to fall, improve, almost**.

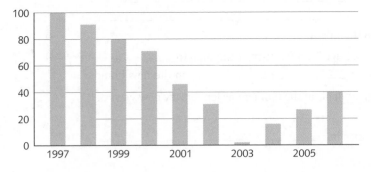

_____

_____

→ Now check your answers in the key.

35 factor something in; factor something into something

Study Read these sentences carefully.

- ▶ They forgot to **factor in** the labour costs when they calculated the price.
- ▶ Insurance is another expense, so make sure that you **factor** it **in**.
- ▶ Inflation must be **factored in** when estimating profits.
- ▶ Usually retailers **factor** the credit card company's fee **into** their prices.
- ▶ The new prices have already **been factored into** our profit forecast.

Check

Use the sentences in the Study box to help you do these exercises.

MEANING

Choose the best meaning of **factor something in**.

- a to reduce an amount when you are calculating something
- b to increase an amount when you are calculating something
- c to include a particular amount when you are calculating something

→ Now check your answers in the key.

GRAMMAR

There is an error in **one** of these sentences. Find it and correct it.

- a They factored in these costs.
- b They factored these costs in.
- c They factored them in.
- d These costs are factored in.
- e These costs are factored in their calculations.

Practise

1 Write the correct preposition, **in** or **into**, in these sentences:

- a We made a mistake and didn't factor _____ all the costs.
- b The bad news has already been factored _____ the share price.
- c Investors have already factored _____ the possibility of an interest rate rise.
- d We have factored all costs, including labour and transport, _____ the estimate.

2 Replace the words <u>underlined</u> with the correct form of **factor in/into**.

- a The possible cost of a merger **has been included in** our calculations.

   _____

- b It is important **to include** interest payments when you work out how much a loan costs.

   _____

- c The cost of materials **should be included** when calculating production costs.

   _____

→ Now check your answers in the key.

Build your vocabulary

OPPOSITES   To **factor out** a cost or expense means 'to deliberately not include it in a calculation':
   ▶ *When inflation is **factored out**, the trade deficit fell by 4%.*

36 fall through

- The deal **fell through** so we had to look for another partner.
- The sale will **fall through** if the buyer pulls out.
- Our plans have **fallen through**.
- We will have to abandon the project if the funding **falls through**.

Check

Use the sentences in the Study box to help you do these exercises.

MEANING

If a deal, plan, sale, etc. **falls through**, what happens?

a It is successful.
b It fails to happen.
c It does not make a lot of money.

GRAMMAR

Which of these are grammatically possible?

a The deal fell through.
b The deal was fallen through.
c The deal has fallen through.
d The deal might fall through.

→ Now check your answers in the key.

Practise

1 Read the text and answer the questions.

A proposed deal between the management and the union over a change in working hours has fallen through for a second time. Last month, the deal fell through as the union refused to accept the extra money offered by the management. After meeting their demands, the management hoped to close the deal this month but have hit another problem, this time over the question of sick pay.

a How many times has the deal failed?

_____

b Why did the deal not succeed last month?

_____

c Why has the deal fallen through again?

_____

2 Fill the spaces with the correct form of **fall through**.

a The deal will _____ if more money is not found.
b The plans have _____ because a sponsor could not be found.
c The sale is likely to _____ .
d The takeover bid _____ last year.
e Our plans _____ because of lack of money.

3 Have you been involved in a deal or a project that failed? Write one or two sentences about it using a form of **fall through** in each.

_____

_____

→ Now check your answers in the key.

37 fill somebody in (on something)

Study Read these sentences carefully.

▸ Has anyone **filled** the customer **in on** what's happened?
▸ There's a slight problem. I'll **fill** you **in on** the details later.
▸ If I miss a meeting, Alison always **fills** me **in**.
▸ The team need to be **filled in on** the new developments.

Check

Use the sentences in the Study box to help you do these exercises.

MEANING

If you **fill somebody in** do you:

a give them a job?
b do their job for them?
c tell them the latest news about something?
d ask them questions?

GRAMMAR

One of these sentences contains a grammatical mistake. Find it and correct it.

a Can someone fill me in?
b Can someone fill James in?
c Has James been filled on what's happened?
d Can someone fill him in?

→ Now check your answers in the key.

Practise

1 Put the words in the right order to make a sentence

a I fill will news you on in the _____

b me she what filled happened in on _____

c me the can in details you the on fill meeting of? _____

2 Match each sentence on the left with a suitable sentence on the right.

a I'll be back in the office by 12.30.
b I'm not sure exactly what was agreed.
c This is just a short note with the basic facts.
d Tim doesn't know much about the project.

i I'll fill you in on the details later.
ii He'll need to be filled in on what we're planning to do.
iii Can you fill me in over lunch?
iv Nobody has filled me in yet.

3 Respond to these questions, using a form of **fill somebody in** and any other words you need.

a Have you heard about what happened in the meeting?

Yes, Alan's _____

b Is there a problem with my order?

Yes, I'll ask the sales manager to _____

→ Now check your answers in the key.

Build your vocabulary

SYNONYMS   To **update somebody (on something)** or to **give somebody an update (on something)** mean the same as to **fill somebody in (on something)**:

▸ *Can you **update me on** what's been going on?*
▸ *Fred **gave me an update on** the latest sales results.*

38 fill in for somebody

Study Read these sentences carefully.

▸ I'm **filling in for** Joe while he's sick.
▸ Mary's on a training course this week. Can you **fill in for** her?
▸ He did a great job when he **filled in for** his boss.

Check

Use the sentences in the Study box to help you do these exercises.

MEANING

Choose the correct word to complete the meaning of **fill in for somebody**:

to do someone else's *letter/job* for a *short/long* time because they are *away/unemployed*

GRAMMAR

Which of these are grammatically possible?

a Jack filled in for Pam.
b Jack filled in for her.
c Jack filled her in while she was away.
d Jack filled in on her.

→ Now check your answers in the key.

Practise

1 Rewrite the part of each sentence in *italics* using an appropriate form of **fill in for** and any other words you need:

a Ian is sick. Can someone *do his work while he is away*?

_____

b Who's going to *do my work* while I'm on vacation?

_____

c I don't usually work on reception. I'm just *covering for a secretary* who is in hospital.

_____

d Thank you for *taking over from Joy* and running the course at such short notice.

_____

2 Read these headlines and say what you think the articles are about.

a Temporary workers fill in for striking employees.

_____

b Grandmother fills in for working parents.

_____

→ Now check your answers in the key.

Build your vocabulary

SYNONYMS **Stand in for somebody** and **cover for somebody** mean the same as **fill in for somebody** and are used in the same way:

▸ Bob **stood in for** me at the meeting.
▸ My boss asked me to **cover for** Mary while she was away.

Note also this use of **fill in**, which has the same meaning:

▸ Mr Jones has been **filling in as** chief executive since June.

39 firm up something

- ▸ The bank is expected to **firm up** plans later in the year.
- ▸ We are looking at all the issues before **firming up** our offer.
- ▸ The sale price has been discussed but the company still has to **firm** it **up**.
- ▸ The details of the agreement haven't been **firmed up** yet.

Check

Use the sentences in the Study box to help you do these exercises.

MEANING

If you **firm up something**, what do you do? Choose the best meaning.

a You change the details of an agreement or a plan.
b You make an agreement, a plan, etc. more definite.

GRAMMAR

There is a grammatical mistake in *one* of these sentences. Find it and correct it.

a The details have been firmed up.
b We need to firm up the details.
c The details have been discussed but we need to firm up them.

→ Now check your answers in the key.

Practise

1 Choose the correct form of **firm up** to fill the gaps in the sentences. You will not need to use them all.

> firm up   firming up   firmed up   firmed it up
> firms up   will firm up   firming it up   firm it up

a The details of the plan will be _____ later.

b The company is currently _____ plans for expansion.

c We have a schedule for the changes but we need to _____ .

d 50% of businesses have already set their marketing budgets; the rest _____ their plans later.

e There's a lot to do for the meeting – papers to prepare, lunch to order, arrangements to _____ .

2 Write a suitable answer to these questions using a form of **firm up something**.

a Does your company have any definite plans for expansion?
   Yes, we are _____

b Have you worked out the details of the agreement yet?
   No, it _____

→ Now check your answers in the key.

Build your vocabulary

SYNONYMS   To **finalize something** can be used with the same meaning:
   ▸ *The details of the contract have not yet been **finalized**.*

40 focus on something

Check

Use the sentences in the Study box to help you do these exercises.

MEANING

If you **focus on something**, which one of the following is most likely to be true?

a you ask for advice
b you give most of your attention to it
c you write a report about it

GRAMMAR

Which of these are grammatically possible?

a We need to focus on the issue.
b We need to focus on it.
c We need to focus it on.
d We need to focus the issue on.

→ Now check your answers in the key.

Practise

1 Match the two halves to make complete sentences.

a The retailer plans to
b The store has
c This month the magazine
d The sales team is

i focuses on product development.
ii focus on attracting male shoppers.
iii focusing on selling digital TV services.
iv focused on expanding the choice of products available.

2 Answer the following questions in full sentences, using an appropriate form of **focus on**, the phrase in brackets and any other words you need.

a What is the main thing the business needs to do?

It needs _____ *(increasing profits)*

b What will be discussed in the meeting?

The meeting _____ *(recruitment of staff)*

c What is the main topic of the report?

_____ *(staff development)*

d What was the subject of the research?

_____ *(the problems faced by small businesses)*

→ Now check your answers in the key.

Build your vocabulary

RELATED WORDS ADJECTIVE: **focused on** or **focussed on**:
- *The management is fully **focussed on** the future.*

IDIOMS It is common to use a phrase such as **focus your attention/efforts/ energy/resources on something** with the same meaning:
- *Over the last two years they have started to **focus their resources on** their biggest brands.*

41 go down; go up

Study Read these sentences carefully.

▶ Costs **are going down**.
▶ Sales **have gone down** 3% in the last year.
▶ The tax **will go up** from 40% to 50%.
▶ The cost of living **went up** by 3.5%.
▶ Food prices **have gone up**.

Check

Use the sentences in the Study box to help you do these exercises.

MEANING

Costs, **sales** and **prices** can **go down** or **go up**. Can you think of *three* more things that can **go down** or **go up**?

_____

_____

_____

GRAMMAR

Which of these are grammatically possible?

a Sales went up.
b Sales are going up.
c Sales were gone up.
d Sales went down this year.
e Sales have gone down.

→ Now check your answers in the key.

Practise

1 Rewrite the following sentences using **go down** or **go up**, so that the meaning stays the same.

a Prices are expected to increase.

b The yen has fallen in value by 5%.

c Inflation is now falling.

d We are trying to prevent our costs from rising.

2 Choose *three* of the words or phrases below and write a sentence using each of them and a form of the verb **go down** or **go up**.

income tax	inflation	sales of …	the cost of …	the price of …	interest rates

a _____
b _____
c _____

→ Now check your answers in the key.

Build your vocabulary

SIMILAR VERBS   →   BE DOWN, BE UP on page 5

42 go under

Study Read these sentences carefully.

- ► He couldn't stop his company from **going under**.
- ► The firm will **go under** unless business improves.
- ► During the recession, more than 10 000 firms **went under**.
- ► Several banks have **gone under** this year, with debts of billions of dollars.

Check

Use the sentences in the Study box to help you do these exercises.

MEANING

If a company **goes under** does it:

a open a new factory in Australia?
b become less successful?
c fail?
d start doing illegal work?

GRAMMAR

Which of the following are grammatically correct?

a The company went under.
b The company went itself under
c The company went under it.
d The company was gone under.
e The company has gone under.

→ Now check your answers in the key.

Practise

1 Match the two halves to make complete sentences.

a Good and bad companies are going under
b If you think your business might go under
c Several airlines went under
d One of our major customers went under
e Many high income businesses have gone under

i when the demand for flights fell.
ii because of the recession.
iii because their expenses were too high.
iv owing us a large amount of money.
v you should get professional advice.

2 Complete these sentences in any way you like, using the verb **go under** in each.

a Jobs are being lost and more and more companies

_____

b I worked for a sports manufacturer until

_____

c If spending levels do not increase soon

_____

d Several small stores in the town _____ since

_____

e If you don't keep up with technology, _____

→ Now check your answers in the key.

43 hammer out something

Study Read these sentences carefully.

▶ Oil producers met to **hammer out** a deal to prevent prices from falling.
▶ A group of employees has **hammered out** a mission statement for the company.
▶ They finally reached an agreement but it had taken a long time to **hammer** it **out**.
▶ A new contract is being **hammered out** between the two sides.

Check

Use the sentences in the Study box to help you do these exercises.

MEANING

Use the words below to complete this meaning of **hammer something out**.

> great   discuss   long   agreed   details

to _____ a plan, deal, etc. for a _____ time and with
_____ effort, until all the _____ are _____

GRAMMAR

Which of these are grammatically possible?

a They are hammering out an
   agreement.
b They are hammering out it.

c They are hammering it out.
d An agreement was hammered out.

→ Now check your answers in the key.

Practise

1 Complete the sentences using an appropriate form of **hammer out**:

a Managers are meeting with the insurance company to _____ a deal.

b The bank's lawyers finally _____ an agreement last year.

c The final details have yet to be _____ .

d They hope to _____ some kind of compromise.

2 Complete the answers to the following questions, using a form of **hammer out**, one of the objects below and any other words you need.

> agreement   final details   rescue package   marketing strategy

a How will the company get out of its financial difficulties?
   Directors are meeting with government officials to

   _____

b How will the new product be advertised?
   We do not know because _____

c Have you presented your business plan to the bank yet?
   No, I'm still _____

→ Now check your answers in the key.

44 hand something **over** (**to** somebody); **hand over** (**to** somebody)

Study Read these sentences carefully.
- He **handed over** his business to his daughter.
- Because she was ill, she had to **hand** the case **over** to her assistant.
- She enjoyed the responsibility and was unwilling to **hand** it **over**.
- Control of the company will be **handed over** at the end of the year.
- Jim Bell **hands over** to the new Chief Executive next month.

Check

Use the sentences in the Study box to help you do these exercises.

MEANING

Choose the best explanation of the meaning of **hand something over** or **hand over** .

a you give control of something or responsibility for something to someone else

b you take control from them and start to do something yourself

GRAMMAR

Which of these are grammatically possible?

a He handed over to his son.
b He handed over control to his son.
c He handed control over to his son.
d He handed over it.
e He handed it over.

→ Now check your answers in the key.

Practise

1 Fill in the gaps in the sentences with a suitable form of **hand something over** or **hand over**.

a She _____ the day-to-day operations of the company to her brother.

b The management was forced to _____ a third of the business.

c The firm has been _____ to a team of accountants.

2 Write a sentence using each of the nouns below and a suitable form of **hand something over (to somebody)** and any other words you like. The first one has been done as an example.

the business   responsibility   the director's job

a *I'm planning to hand over the business to my son when he's 25.*

b _____

c _____

→ Now check your answers in the key.

Build your vocabulary

RELATED WORDS   NOUN: **handover.** This is a countable noun, usually singular.
- *The **handover** of power took place two years ago.*

IDIOMS   **Hand over the reins (to somebody)** means 'to give power or control to somebody':
- *It was time to **hand over the reins to** his assistant.*

SIMILAR VERBS   → TURN SOMETHING OVER TO SOMEBODY on page 98

45 head up something

Check

Use the sentences in the Study box to help you do these exercises.

MEANING

Which of the following best explains the meaning of **head up**?

a to be moving up in a company or a department
b to be in charge of a company or a department
c to change the company or department that you work for

GRAMMAR

Which of these are grammatically possible?

a Max heads up the marketing department.
b Max heads it up.
c The marketing department is headed up by Max.
d Max heads the marketing department up.
e Max heads me up.

→ Now check your answers in the key.

Practise

1 Look at the diagram of the company's organizational structure, then say which of the statements are true or false. Correct any that are false.

a Liz Jacobs heads up the sales team.
b Ann Smith heads up the company.
c Brian Tate heads up the production department.
d The IT department is headed up by Tim Jones.

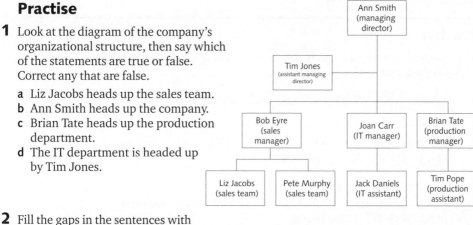

2 Fill the gaps in the sentences with the correct form of **head up**.

a He would like _____ the sales team.

b She is going _____ our branch in the US.

c Will the project _____ by someone from outside the company?

d This is Mark. He _____ our design team.

→ Now check your answers in the key.

Build your vocabulary

SIMILAR VERBS → REPORT TO on page 71

46 hire something or somebody out

Study Read these sentences carefully.

- ▶ He owns a business that **hires out** building tools.
- ▶ I'm looking for a company that **hires** photocopiers **out**.
- ▶ Half of the equipment that was **hired out** was unusable.
- ▶ Our business is **hiring out** technical staff.
- ▶ I contacted the agency that **hired** her **out** to us.
- ▶ He **hires** himself **out** as a bodyguard.

Check

Use the sentences in the Study box to help you do these exercises.

MEANING

If you **hire out** equipment, what do you do?

a You pay to use it for a short period of time.

b You allow someone to use it for a short time in return for payment.

GRAMMAR

There is a gramamtical mistake in *one* of these sentences. Find it and correct it.

a The company hires out secretarial staff.

b The company hires them out.

c The company hires out them.

d Secretarial staff are hired out on a daily rate.

→ Now check your answers in the key.

Practise

1 Read these adverts then complete the sentences using a form of **hire out** to say what these companies do.

a ADAM'S AUTOS: WE HAVE CARS FOR ALL OCCASIONS

_____

b CAMDEN CATERING COMPANY: SUPPLIERS OF CHEFS AND WAITING STAFF FOR WEDDINGS, CONFERENCES, ETC.

_____

c THAMES TEMPS: TEMPORARY SECRETARIAL AND OFFICE STAFF ON SHORT OR MEDIUM TERM BASIS

_____

2 Complete these sentences with an appropriate form of **hire out** and one of the objects below.

both Apple Macs and PCs   interpreters   cameras   herself

a If you don't have your own computer, there are several companies that

_____

b She _____ as an after-dinner speaker.

c We _____ to film companies.

d Our company _____ for international conferences.

→ Now check your answers in the key.

47 hold up

Study Read these sentences carefully.

▸ Levels of exports are still **holding up**.
▸ Sales have **held up** well in recent months in spite of economic difficulties.
▸ Sales for the third quarter **held up** better than expected
▸ She's **holding up** well under pressure.

Check

Use the sentences in the Study box to help you do these exercises.

MEANING

Choose the best explanation of this meaning of **hold up**:

a to delay something
b to pick something up
c to stay strong

GRAMMAR

Which of these are grammatically possible?

a They held up prices.
b Prices held up.
c Prices held themselves up.
d He held up well.

→ Now check your answers in the key.

Practise

1 Which *three* phrases in the following text could be replaced with a form of **hold up**?

> Market conditions have been difficult recently, but our profits have remained solid. We have been helped by the fact that the euro has kept its value against the dollar over the last six months. In general, in spite of problems in the global market, demand for our goods has continued at the same level and has even increased slightly.

_____

_____

_____

2 Fill the gaps with an appropriate form of **hold up**.

a The economy is _____ better than expected.

b We forecast that consumer stocks will _____ well in the short term.

c Last year, public sector spending _____ better than in the private sector.

d Exports have _____ in recent weeks in a market that is slowing down.

e Sales _____ well last month.

3 Complete the following dialogues using a form of **hold up**.

a Has the value of the euro fallen?
    No, it seems to be _____

b The sales figures look quite good this month.
    Yes, sales have _____ well over the last three months.

c Are you worried about the economy?
    No, our economy is _____ despite the world recession.

→ Now check your answers in the key.

48 hook something or somebody up (to something)

Study Read these sentences carefully.

- ▸ You can **hook** your laptop **up** to a big screen when you give your presentation.
- ▸ Did you remember to **hook up** the loudspeaker system?
- ▸ If you bring your own keyboard, you can **hook** it **up** to my PC.
- ▸ The computers are all **hooked up** to a central server.

Check

Use the sentences in the Study box to help you do these exercises.

MEANING

Use the words below to complete this meaning of **hook up**.

| supply | equipment | connect | electrical |

to _____ a computer or a

piece of _____ equipment

to another piece of _____

or a power _____

GRAMMAR

Which of these are grammatically possible?

- a We hooked the computer up.
- b We hooked up the computer.
- c We hooked it up.
- d We hooked up it.
- e The computers are hooked up.

→ Now check your answers in the key.

Practise

1 Complete the following sentences using *two* words in each one.

- a All the PCs here are hooked _____ the Internet.
- b She brought her own laptop in and hooked _____ to our network.
- c We hooked the camera _____ a computer to store the images.

2 Rewrite the parts of the sentences in **italics** using an appropriate form of **hook up** and any other words that you need.

- a I've brought my PC. Do you mind if I *plug it in*?

  _____

- b For some reason this machine *isn't connected to* a printer.

  _____

- c We have eighteen computers *connected to* the Internet.

  _____

- d I heard he *had connected a tape recorder to his telephone* so he could record calls.

  _____

→ Now check your answers in the key.

Build your vocabulary

RELATED WORDS   NOUN: **hook-up** (= a connection between two computers or pieces of electrical equipment:) (This is a countable noun.)

- ▸ *They were able to talk to each other via a satellite* **hook-up**.

49 hook up (with somebody)

Study Read these sentences carefully.

▶ Two of Europe's leading fashion designers have **hooked up** to produce this range of clothing.
▶ We've **hooked up** with a firm in Germany to make the printers.
▶ The two men will probably **hook up** as equal partners in the business.

Check

Use the sentences in the Study box to help you do these exercises.

MEANING

If two companies **hook up**, what do they do? Only *one* answer is correct.

a They work together for a period of time.
b They combine to form one company.
c They compete with each other.

GRAMMAR

Which of these are grammatically possible?

a They hooked up with a UK company.
b The two companies hooked up.
c They were hooked up with a UK company.
d We hooked the company up.

→ Now check your answers in the key.

Practise

1 Correct the following sentences by deleting *one* word from each sentence.

a They have hooked it up with a leading telecommunications company to develop the new technology.
b The two companies hooked up with in order to combine their expertise.
c Both companies saw sales rise when they were hooked up last year.

2 Complete the following sentences by adding an appropriate form of **hook up** and **with** where necessary.

a We could improve sales by _____ a specialist marketing company.

b They are keen _____ a distribution company that knows the local markets.

c Two airlines have _____ to offer cheap holidays in Europe.

d She _____ a partner to build a children's clothing company.

e It's difficult if one firm wants _____ but the other isn't interested.

→ Now check your answers in the key.

Build your vocabulary

RELATED WORDS   NOUN: **hook-up** (This is a countable noun.)
▶ *They have just agreed a **hook-up** with an American company in an attempt to expand into the US market.*

SYNONYMS   **Team up (with somebody):**
▶ *The two companies **teamed up** to manufacture products for world markets.*

Collaborate (with somebody) is a more formal verb:
▶ *We **collaborate** with suppliers on product design and logistics.*

50 key something in; key something into something

- First, **key in** your password.
- Who **keyed** the information **in**?
- When entering your personal number, **key** it **in** carefully.
- When the data has all been **keyed in**, the paper files can be thrown away.
- You have to **key** a special code **into** the control panel.
- All the information has been **keyed into** the computer.

Check

Use the sentences in the Study box to help you do these exercises.

MEANING

Use two of the words below to complete the meaning of **key in/key into**.

lock   secrets   information
keyboard   key

to put _____

into a computer using a _____

GRAMMAR

There is *one* error in each of these sentences. Find them and correct them.

a She keyed in it.
b She keyed into the computer the data.
c She keyed into the computer it.
d The data was keyed the computer.

→ Now check your answers in the key.

Practise

1 Match the two halves to make complete sentences:

a If you can't get into your file,
  you may have
b He had the boring job of
c Information is
d Text can be viewed on the screen

i as it is keyed in.
ii keyed into the computer
   via a keyboard.
iii keying numbers into a database.
iv keyed in your password incorrectly.

2 Replace the words in *italics* with a form of **key in/into** and any other words you need.

a Can you *enter this data into* the computer?

_____

b I think you may have *entered it into* the database wrongly.

_____

c In most stores, you can now *enter* a four-figure PIN instead of signing your name.

_____

→ Now check your answers in the key.

Build your vocabulary

SYNONYMS   To **type in** means the same as **key in** and is used in the same way:
- *He typed in all the information.*
- *Type the code into the computer.*

The process or job of keying information into a computer is known as **data entry**.
- *Data entry clerks were paid by how fast they keyed in data.*

Human Resources

These phrasal verbs can all be used when you are talking about **Human Resources**:

bring in	burn out	contract out	deal with	fill in for
hand over	lay off	put in	report to	run by
step down	take on	turn over		

Exercise 1 – Be the consultant

**Find a solution for these business problems.
Choose a phrase from the list on the right.**

a **What would you suggest for
a company that...**

1 is experiencing an increase
   in demand for its products.
2 needs to improve its computer systems.
3 has an empty order book.
4 is behind with its orders.

The company should...

a lay staff off
b bring in temporary staff
c take on more staff
d bring in some outside IT experts

b **Now give some personal advice to your colleague who...**

1 feels she is not paid enough.
2 says he no longer has time to go to
   extra meetings.
3 can't attend an important meeting.
4 has an idea for a new sales campaign.

a Step down from the committee.
b Run it by your manager.
c Put in a request for a pay rise.
d Ask your deputy to fill in for you.

Exercise 2 – Synonyms

**Replace the phrasal verb in each sentence with one of the expressions in the box.
Remember to change the form of the verb if necessary.**

hand over   make redundant   outsource   recruit   stand in for   stand down

1 Wingworks Ltd are **taking on** more staff for the summer period. _____

2 Who will be **filling in for** Mrs Taylor while she's away? _____

3 The founder of the firm, Dan T. Gabriel, decided to **step down**
   and **turn** the running of the company **over** to his son, Archie. _____

4 We don't do our own printing.
   We **contract** it **out** to a firm in Asia. _____

5 When the recession hit, the factory **laid off** 100 workers. _____

Exercise 3 – Test yourself

Match the beginnings and endings to make sentences.

1 He felt he was burned out
2 They're bringing in a new sales manager
3 I report to Ann Jefferson
4 If you put in your expenses claim today

a and I'll have to run the idea by her.
b so he decided to step down as CEO.
c I'll deal with it tomorrow.
d to take over from Alan Stewart.

The life of a company

These phrasal verbs can all be used to describe the life of a company:

branch out	break up	build up	buy out	close down	cut back	go under
open up	sell off	start up	take on	take over	wind up	

Exercise 1 – Patterns of meaning

Put the phrasal verbs into the following categories according to their meaning. Sometimes, a verb will fit into more than one category. The first one has been done for you as an example.

begin	end	expand	reduce
		branch out	

Exercise 2

a Arrange the following phrasal verbs in the order in which you think they are most likely to happen when somebody starts a new company. The first one has been done for you as an example:

branch out	____
break up	____
build up	____
close down	____
cut back	____
go under	____
open up	____
sell off	____
start up	*1*
wind up	____

b Now put the verbs in the correct form to fill the gaps in the text:

Six years ago, Mike ¹ ___started up___ his own business selling cameras. The company was a great success and he ² _____ stores all over the UK. He had ³ _____ a good relationship with his bank and so they agreed to lend him the money to expand and ⁴ _____ into selling computers.

Unfortunately the computers were not popular. Profits fell sharply and Mike realized that he had to make dramatic changes. He started to ⁵ _____ on spending and ⁶ _____ his less profitable stores. Profits continued to fall however, so he decided to ⁷ _____ the company in order to ⁸ _____ his computer division. Then the bank demanded their money back and there was no way to stop the firm ⁹ _____. He was finally forced to ¹⁰ _____ operations completely.

Exercise 3 – Related words

Rewrite the following sentences so that the meaning stays the same, using a form of the related phrasal verb and any other words you need. The first one has been done for you as an example:

1 The company's **start-up** costs came to around $2 million.

It cost _around $2 million to start up the new company._

2 The airline has announced details of the planned **takeover** of its rival.

The airline has announced its plans _____

3 The government is planning the **break-up** of the state-owned phone company.

The government is planning to _____

4 In the current situation, staff **cutbacks** will be necessary.

In the current situation we will have to _____

5 The firm has announced the **sell-off** of most of its American bus operation.

The firm has announced that _____

6 Serious unemployment followed the **close-down** of several factories in the area.

There was serious unemployment when _____

Exercise 4 – Synonyms and similar verbs

Use one of the phrasal verbs from the box to replace the words in **bold** in the following sentences.
You may need to change the form of these words.

prop up   beat off   bring out   close down   sell off

1 The company **came out with** its latest model in July.
2 The hotel chain is trying to **fight off** a hostile bid from a Singapore property company.
3 State aid was used to **bail out** failing businesses.
4 Some of the firm's buildings and vehicles have now been **auctioned off**.
5 The factory **shut down** last year.

Exercise 5 – Test yourself

Match the two halves to make complete sentences

a She resigned her position as managing director and...
b Profits were falling until we decided to branch out...
c The board of directors has agreed to...
d The phone company was ...
e The new laws will...

1 started up her own media company.
2 open up the country to foreign investment.
3 buy out the two main shareholders.
4 taken over by a multinational electronics firm.
5 into computer games as well.

Describing trends

These phrasal verbs can all be used to describe economic or financial trends:

be down	be up	bottom out	drop off	dry up	go down	go up
hold up	level off	mount up	pick up	take off	turn down	

Exercise 1 – Patterns of meaning

Put the phrasal verbs from the list above into the following categories according to their meaning. The first one has been done for you as an example:

move upwards	move downwards	stay in the same position
be up		

Exercise 2

Look at the line graph showing sales of a book in the year 2004. First, replace the bold phrases in each sentence below with one of the phrasal verbs from the box at the top of this page and then complete the sentence by looking at the data on the graph itself. The first one has been done for you as an example:

book sales 2004

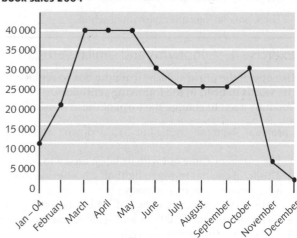

1 Sales **reached their lowest point** in _____ .

   Sales bottomed out in December.

2 Sales **rose dramatically** from the beginning of _____ .

3 After their sharp rise sales **stayed strong** from _____ to _____ .

4 Sales **increased** by 100% in _____ .

5 Sales **stopped increasing or decreasing** from _____ to _____ .

6 Sales **fell steadily** from the beginning of _____ .

7 Sales **improved** a little in _____ .

8 Sales **remained high** in _____ and _____ .

9 Sales **started to fall** for the first time at the beginning of _____ .

10 By the beginning of _____ , sales had almost **disappeared completely**.

Arrangements and Negotiations

These phrasal verbs can be used to talk about making arrangements and negotiating deals.

break down	bring forward	draw up	fall through	firm up
hammer out	pencil in	pull out (of)	put together	set up

Exercise 1 – Patterns of meaning

Decide which are most useful for each topic:

Preparing a meeting and fixing a date	Preparing or organizing sth	Negotiating a deal or failure to agree

Exercise 2

Put this phone conversation into the right order, so that it makes sense:

a OK, and I'll draw up the agenda and email it to you.
b Yes, that should be possible. Shall we pencil in May 18, then?
c Hello, Jim. I'm ringing to set up our meeting about the joint project. Would the last week in May suit you?
d Fine, I'll call you nearer the time to firm up the date.
e I'm not sure - I may have to go to a conference on May 25. Could we bring it forward a week?

Exercise 3

Use the verbs from the 'Negotiating' box to fill the gaps in this news report. Remember to change the forms of the verbs if necessary.

In other news, talks _____ last night between

unions and management at the Cheetah car factory. It had been

hoped that the two sides would be able to _____ an

agreement, but the deal _____ when the unions

_____ the negotiations, saying that the

new offer did not represent an improvement.

Up

Many of the verbs in this book combine with **up**.

Exercise 1 – Patterns of meaning

You may be able to see some patterns of meaning of these verbs. Write each of the verbs in the box below in the correct column according to its meaning. You can look back at the main pages to help you.

draw up	drum up	dry up	mount up	open up	pay up
pick up	set up	smarten up	start up	wind up	

Increasing/improving	Making ready	Ending

Exercise 2 – Synonyms

Choose the verb from the boxes which means the same as the bold verb in each of these sentences. You will not need to use all of them.

team up with	settle up	raise	put up	shore up	play	run up

a You must **bring up** the issue with your line manager.   _____

b We need to **pay up** before we leave.   _____

c The company had **accumulated** large debts.   _____

d New investors are required to **prop up** the business.   _____

e German researchers will **hook up with** Japanese researchers. _____

Exercise 3 – Opposites

Draw a line to join each phrasal verb with its opposite.

tie up   go down   open up   close down   free up   go up

Now rewrite the sentences so that the meaning stays the same, using one verb from each pair in the correct form:

a The store stopped trading.

b A new store started trading

c Prices are increasing.

d Prices became lower.

e Something is preventing the money from being available.

f The sale of assets has allowed more money to become available.

a The store _____ .

b A new store _____ .

c Prices _____ .

d Prices _____ .

e Something _____ the money.

f The sale of assets _____ more money.

Exercise 4 –Related words

Choose the correct verb and then form it into a noun or an adjective to fill the gap in each sentence. You will need to use one of them more than once.

| mark up   start up   shake up   back up   break up |

a Make a _____ of all files onto a floppy disk.

b The _____ on clothes is often as high as 80%.

c Forty people lost their jobs in the recent _____ .

d The _____ costs of the new company had been relatively small.

e The eight partners gave £1 million to fund the _____ .

f The _____ of a firm after a failed merger is not unknown.

Exercise 5 –Test yourself

Test your knowledge of these verbs by completing the sentences with a verb in the correct form. Try to do this without looking back at the pages of verbs.

A German businessman ^{1}_____ the money, and three years ago we ^{2}_____ an office in Bonn. We sent out lots of mail in order to try to ^{3}_____ some business. For the first few months, sales were poor but then things started to ^{4}_____ . Sales have continued to ^{5}_____ and now we are making a comfortable profit.

Exercise 6

Choose the best verb to fit in the space in each sentence.

a Sales _____ up for the third year running.

    are   put   set

b We're hoping to _____ up a network of contacts.

    build   smarten   wind

c Several people have already _____ up for the course.

    stocked   picked   signed

d The company needs to _____ up its image.

    smarten   mount   firm

e All the money is _____ up in investments.

    tied   hooked   stocked

f She will _____ up a team of researchers.

    shake   head   bring

g Business _____ up and the company was forced to close.

    dried   tied   marked

R7

Out

Many of the verbs in this book combine with **out**.

Exercise 1 – Patterns of meaning

You may be able to see some patterns of meaning of these verbs. Write each of the verbs below in the correct column according to its meaning. You can look back at the main pages to help you.

bring out	burn out	buy out	hire out
pull out	phase out	roll out	turn out

Making available	Ending or completing

Exercise 2 – Synonyms

Choose the verb from the box that means the same as the verb in these sentences. Then rewrite the sentences using the verbs you have chosen.

contract out	branch out	bottom out	pull out

a Production levelled off last year.

_____

b Cleaning and catering are being outsourced.

_____

c The company backed out of the deal at the last minute.

_____

d We decided to diversify and start selling CDs as well as books.

_____

Exercise 3 – Related words

Fill the gap in each sentence with a noun related to the phrasal verb in brackets.

i   The initial _____ on equipment was very high. (**lay something out**)

ii   There's a high level of stress and _____ among teachers. (**burn yourself out**)

iii The event was held to mark the _____ of the new product.
     (**roll something out**)

iv   The _____ of the unpopular tax will happen over the next five years.
     (**phase something out**)

Exercise 4 – Test yourself

Match each verb with its definition. Try to do this without looking back at the pages of phrasal verbs.

carry sth out

lay sth out

contract sth out

phase sth out

hammer sth out

bring sth out

a to gradually stop using something or stop providing it

b to do something that you need to plan and organize

c to spend money on something, especially a lot of money

d to pay someone outside your company to do some work for you

e to discuss the details of something such as a business deal

f to make a new product available for people to buy

Exercise 5

Complete these sentences with one of the verbs in exercise 4 in the correct form.

a We were unable to do the work in-house so we decided to _____ it out.

b The system was unworkable so it was gradually _____ out.

c The company _____ huge sums of money on new machinery last year.

d The study was _____ out by researchers in Germany.

e I heard they had _____ an agreement at the last minute.

f We are considering _____ a new version of the software.

Exercise 6

Rewrite these sentences, replacing the noun or phrase in *italics* with a pronoun such as 'it' or 'them' in the correct position.

a The company brought out *the software* in 2004.

  The company _____

b The hospital plans to contract out *cleaning services*.

  The hospital _____

c He has ruled out *the possibility*.

  _____

Exercise 7

Which word could you *not* use with the phrasal verb next to it?

a **carry out** research an investigation a deal

b **hire out** equipment machinery an idea

c **phase out** a system a tax an office

d **lay out** money staff resources

Test yourself

You have studied other verbs which have not been included in the other review pages. Use this page to test yourself on these verbs.

Exercise 1

Choose the correct verb to fill the space in each sentence.

a The money could be invested to _____ in a regular income.

   cash   **bring**   **fill**

b Huge losses will have to be _____ off.

   written   **beaten**   **dropped**

c He wasn't ready to _____ on such a big responsibility.

   focus   **take**   **bring**

d Customers will continue to _____ around for the best price.

   turn   **play**   **shop**

e I can't see the idea _____ on with people in business.

   catching   **taking**   **focusing**

f The costs can be _____ down into two categories.

   turned   **closed**   **broken**

g Back injuries _____ for thousands of lost working days every year.

   account   **fall**   **report**

h Rising employment costs should be _____ in when calculating the budget.

   brought   **keyed**   **factored**

Exercise 2

Match the verb in *italics* with a phrasal verb in the box which means the same. You will not need to use all the phrasal verbs.

| cash in on sth | copy sb in | bring sb in | fill sb in | key sth in |

a Could you *update* me on what's been happening while I've been away?
b He was busy *typing in* all the data.
c Many companies have *profited from* the situation.

Exercise 3

Complete the following sentences with a noun or an adjective that is related to the phrasal verbs in the box.

| break sth down | focus on sth | dispose of sth | rip off sb |

a Could you give me a _____ of the figures?

b We need a more _____ approach.

c Many of the products are poor quality and a _____ .

d The _____ of assets helped bring the company back into profitability.

Review pages – answer key

Human Resources

Exercise 1a
1 c   2 d   3 a   4 b

Exercise 1b
1 c   2 a   3 d   4 b

Exercise 2
1 … are recruiting …
2 … be standing in for …
3 … to stand down and hand the running of the company over to his son …
4 We outsource it…
5 … made 100 workers redundant.

Exercise 3
1 b   2 d   3 a   4 c

The life of a company

Exercise 1

Begin	end	expand	reduce
open up	close down	*branch out*	cut back
start up	break up	build up	sell off
	go under	take on	(break up)
	sell off	take over	
	wind up	(buy out)	
	(buy out)		

Exercise 2a
Start up 1
open up 2
build up 3
branch out 4
cut back 5
close down 6
break up 7
sell off 8
go under 9
wind up 10

Exercise 2b
1 *started up*
2 opened up
3 built up
4 branch out
5 cut back
6 close down
7 break up
8 sell off
9 going under
10 wind up

Exercise 3
1 It cost around $2 million to start up the new company.
2 The airline has announced its plans to take over its rival.
3 The government is planning to break up the state-owned phone company.
4 In the current situation we will have to cut back on staff.
5 The firm has announced that it is selling off its American bus operation.
6 There was serious unemployment when several factories in the area closed down.

Exercise 4
1 brought out
2 beat off
3 prop up
4 sold off
5 closed down

Exercise 5
a 1   b 5   c 3   d 4   e 2

Describing Trends

Exercise 1

Move upwards	move downwards	stay in the same position
be up	be down	bottom out
go up	drop off	hold up
mount up	dry up	level off
pick up	go down	
take off	turn down	
	(bottom out)	

Exercise 2
1 *Sales bottomed out in December.*
2 Sales took off from the beginning of February.
3 Sales held up/levelled off from March to May.
4 Sales went up by 100% in February.
5 Sales levelled off from July to September.
6 Sales went down from the beginning of May.
7 Sales picked up in September.
8 Sales held up in July and August.
9 Sales started to drop off/turn down/go down at the beginning of May.
10 By the beginning of December sales had almost dried up.

Arrangements and Negotiations

Exercise 1

Preparing a meeting	preparing or organizing something	negotiating a deal or failure to agree
bring forward	draw up	break down
pencil in	(firm up)	fall through
set up	put together	hammer out
(firm up)		pull out
		(firm up)

Exercise 2
c   e   b   d   a

Exercise 3

In other news, talks **broke down** last night between unions and management at the Cheetah car factory. It had been hoped that the two sides would be able to **hammer out** an agreement, but the deal **fell through** when the unions **pulled out of** the negotiations, saying that the new offer did not represent an improvement.

Up

Exercise 1

Increasing /improving	Making ready	Ending
drum up	draw up	dry up
mount up	open up	pay up
pick up	set up	wind up
smarten up	start up	

Exercise 2

a raise
b settle up
c run up
d shore up
e team up with

Exercise 3

tie up – free up
open up – close down
go down – go up

a The store closed down
b A new store opened up.
c Prices are going up.
d Prices went down.
e Something is tying up the money.
f The sale of assets has freed up more money

Exercise 4

a backup
b markup
c shake-up
d start-up
e start-up
f break-up

Exercise 5

A German businessman **put up** the money, and three years ago we **opened up** an office in Bonn. We sent out lots of mail in order to try to **drum up** some business. For the first few months, sales were poor but then things started to **pick up**. Sales have continued to **hold up** /**go up** and now we are making a comfortable profit.

Exercise 6

a are
b build
c signed
d smarten
e tied
f head
g dried

Out

Exercise 1

Making available	ending or completing
bring out	burn out
hire out	buy out
roll out	phase out
turn out	pull out

Exercise 2

a Production bottomed out last year.
b Cleaning and catering are being contracted out.
c The company pulled out of the deal at the last minute.
d We decide to branch out and start selling CDs as well as books.

Exercise 3

i   outlay
ii   burnout
iii roll-out
iv   phase-out

Exercise 4

a phase sth out
b carry sth out
c lay sth out
d contract sth out
e hammer sth out
f bring sth out

Exercise 5

a contract it out
b phased out
c laid out
d carried out
e hammered out
f bringing out

Exercise 6

a The company brought it out in 2004.
b The hospital plans to contract them out.
c He has ruled it out.

Exercise 7

a a deal
b an idea
c an office
d staff

Test Yourself

Exercise 1

a bring
b written
c take
d shop
e catching
f broken
g account
h factored

Exercise 2

a Could you fill me in on what's been happening…?
b He was busy keying in all the data.
c Many companies have cashed in on this situation.

Exercise 3

a Could you give me a breakdown of the figures?
b We need a more focussed approach.
c Many of the products are poor quality and a rip-off.
d The disposal of assets helped…

51 lay somebody off

Study Read these sentences carefully.
▶ The company **laid off** 120 workers last year.
▶ If we lose the contract then we will have to **lay** some staff **off**.
▶ Several people have returned to work for the firm that **laid** them **off**.
▶ He was **laid off** during the recession.

Check

Use the sentences in the Study box to help you do these exercises.

MEANING

What happens if somebody is **laid off**?

a They take a day off work because they are ill.
b They lose their job because the company has problems.
c They get a new job after a long period without one.

GRAMMAR

Which of these are grammatically possible?

a The company laid off the workers.
b The company laid them off.
c The company laid off them.
d The workers were laid off.
e The workers laid off.

→ Now check your answers in the key.

Practise

1 True or False?

a Companies usually lay people off to reduce costs. T / F
b Companies usually lay people off when business is doing well. T / F
c People who are laid off may get their jobs back later. T / F

2 Rewrite the words that are **underlined** using an appropriate form of **lay off**.

a The company will have to **end the jobs of** 150 workers if sales don't improve.

_____

b He **lost his job** when the company closed down his factory.

_____

c They **ended the jobs of** half the workforce due to falling orders.

_____

d We are hoping to avoid closing plants and **getting rid of** staff.

_____

→ Now check your answers in the key.

Build your vocabulary

RELATED WORDS   NOUN: **lay-off** (= the act of dismissing workers because there is not enough work; an example of this) (This is a countable noun.)
▶ *They announced the temporary **lay-off** of 8 000 car workers.*
▶ *500 **lay-offs** were announced in December.*

SYNONYMS   To **make somebody redundant** means the same, but is permanent:
▶ *He was **made redundant** when the factory closed down.*

OPPOSITES   → TAKE SOMBODY ON on page 88

52 lay something out

- They've **laid out** more than $1 million **on** new machinery.
- No one wants to **lay** money **out** without some kind of guarantee.
- We saved more than €15 000 and **laid** it all **out on** a new van.
- A lot of money has already been **laid out**.

Check

Use the sentences in the Study box to help you do these exercises.

MEANING

Which of these verbs means the same as **lay out something**?

a earn
b cost
c spend
d steal

GRAMMAR

Which of these are grammatically possible?

a We've laid out a lot of money on the project.
b A lot of money has been laid out.
c We've laid a lot of money out.
d A lot of money is laying out.

→ Now check your answers in the key.

Practise

1 Choose the correct form of **lay out** from the list to fill the gaps in the sentences. You will not need to use all of them.

lay out	lays out	been laid out	laid out	laying out	was laid out	will lay out

a They have _____ a lot of money on the equipment.

b We will have to _____ about $5 000 on the project.

c Around $60 000 has already _____ on new offices.

d Many firms are _____ vast amounts of money.

e The company _____ €125 000 over the next 3 years.

2 Think about something you have had to spend a lot of money on. Write a sentence using **lay out**, to say what you bought and how much money you spent.

→ Now check your answers in the key.

Build your vocabulary

RELATED WORDS   NOUN: **outlay** means the amount of money that you need to spend on sth, especially a new business or project. It is countable and uncountable.

- *The business required a large initial* **outlay** *on equipment.*

53 level off

Study Read these sentences carefully.
- ▸ Output fell sharply and then **levelled off**.
- ▸ The rate of increase appears to be **levelling off**.
- ▸ There are signs that the growth in sales is starting to **level off**.

Check

Use the sentences in the Study box to help you do these exercises.

MEANING

Answer these questions.

1 If profits level off, are they: a) high; b) low; c) either high or low?
2 If profits level off, were they previously: a) rising; b) falling; c) either of these?

GRAMMAR

One of these sentences is incorrect. Find it and correct the mistake.

a Prices have levelled off.
b Prices have started to level off now.
c Prices have started to level themselves off now.

→ Now check your answers in the key.

Practise

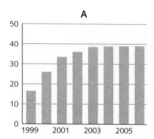
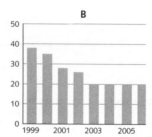
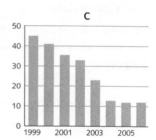

1 When did sales level off in each graph?
A _____ B _____ C _____

2 Now complete the sentences about these graphs, using the correct form of the verbs **rise**, **fall**, and **level off**.

a **Graph A:** Sales _____ between 1999 and _____
   and then _____

b **Graph B:** Sales _____ and then _____

c **Graph C:** Between 1999 and _____ sales _____

→ Now check your answers in the key.

Build your vocabulary

SYNONYMS   **Level out** means the same as **level off** and is used in the same way.

SIMILAR VERBS   → BOTTOM OUT on page 6
This is only used for something that stops *falling* or *decreasing*.

54 lock somebody, something or yourself **into** something; lock somebody, something or yourself **in**

Study Read these sentences carefully.

- I wouldn't recommend **locking** all your money **into** one investment.
- It's not a good idea to **lock** yourself **into** today's interest rates.
- You will be **locked into** the investment for at least ten years.
- We haven't got much money so we don't want to **lock** it **into** a long-term investment.
- She does not want her money to be **locked in** for a long period.

Check

Use the sentences in the Study box to help you do these exercises.

MEANING

If you are **locked into** an agreement, are the following true or false?

a you can't remove your money from the investment when you like **(T/F)**

b you cannot change the details of the agreement for a period of time **(T/F)**

c you can change the details of the agreement **(T/F)**

GRAMMAR

Which of these are grammatically possible?

a He locked himself into the investment.

b He was locked into the investment.

c He locked into the investment.

d His money was locked in.

→ Now check your answers in the key.

Practise

1 Complete the following sentences using the phrases below.

be locked into	locked him into	lock it into	to lock herself into

a She didn't want _____ a mortgage with a fixed interest rate.

b Under this deal, your savings would _____ the investment plan for ten years.

c If you think you will need your money, it isn't a good idea to _____ long-term bonds.

d The company has _____ a long-term contract.

2 Complete the dialogues using an appropriate form of **lock into** or **lock in**.

a Why are investors unwilling to sign up to these long-term agreements?

They don't like to feel that their money _____ very long-term investments.

b Does my money have to be invested for ten or fifteen years?

No, if you don't want to _____ your money for that length of time, you can arrange a shorter period.

→ Now check your answers in the key.

55 mark something up

Study Read these sentences carefully.

▶ If a store faces a lot of competition, it is less likely to **mark up** its prices.
▶ Wholesalers sell goods to stores, which **mark** them **up** for retail.
▶ Some stores had **marked** the game **up** by 10%.
▶ The fruit is heavily **marked up** out of season.

Check

Use the sentences in the Study box to help you do these exercises.

MEANING

Which of these is the best explanation of this meaning of **mark something up**?

a to damage something
b to increase the price of something
c to write a description of something

GRAMMAR

Which of these are grammatically possible?

a They marked up the price.
b They marked it up.
c They marked up it.
d The price was marked up.

→ Now check your answers in the key.

Practise

1 Match the two halves to make complete sentences.

a Companies have to mark up their products
b Steel prices have been marked up by
c The cameras had been marked up

i almost 10%.
ii to $320.
iii to make a profit.

2 Complete the sentences using a form of **mark up** and one of the words or phrases below.

> drinks   prices   their beds

a Many stores took advantage of the change in currency to _____ .

b Most furniture stores _____ by about 20%.

c Restaurants make most of their money from _____ .

→ Now check your answers in the key.

Build your vocabulary

RELATED WORDS   NOUN: **markup** means 'the difference between the cost of producing or buying something and the price it is sold at' (This noun is usually used in the singular.)
▶ *The average **markup** on televisions is 40%.*

OPPOSITES   **mark something down:**
▶ *The PC I wanted had been **marked down** to €700.*

There is also a noun **markdown**:
▶ *We're offering a 10% **markdown** on selected items.*

56 measure up (to/against something)

Check

Use the sentences in the Study box to help you do these exercises.

MEANING

If somebody or something **measures up**, are they:

a large and powerful?
b good enough?
c very expensive?
d the right size?

GRAMMAR

Which of these are grammatically possible?

a The business didn't measure up.
b The business didn't measure it up.
c The business measures up well against others.
d The business measures up to others.

→ Now check your answers in the key.

Practise

1 Choose the correct word to complete each sentence:

a The equipment didn't measure up **to/in** required standards.
b The service measures up **good/well** in comparison to others.
c How does the company measure up **for/against** others?
d They sent out inspectors to check that companies were **measuring/measured** up.

2 Rewrite these sentences by replacing the words that are underlined with an appropriate form of **measure up** and any other words that you need.

a Drivers who <u>are not good enough</u> could be fined.

_____

b How does your firm <u>compare to</u> the best?

_____

c She was trying to <u>be as successful as</u> her parents, who were both senior managers.

_____

d Many companies have failed to <u>deal effectively with</u> the challenges they face.

_____

e How <u>good are</u> your staff?

_____

→ Now check your answers in the key.

57 mount up

- ▶ The bills were **mounting up**.
- ▶ Her expenses **mounted up** fast.
- ▶ The paperwork has been **mounting up** while I've been away.
- ▶ The evidence against him soon **mounted up**.

Check

Use the sentences in the Study box to help you do these exercises.

MEANING

1 Which of the following is closest in meaning to **mount up**?

a to form a pile
b to be reduced in size
c to increase

2 Look at the examples again and write down three things that can **mount up**.

_____

_____

_____

GRAMMAR

Which of these are grammatically possible?

a The costs mounted up.
b The costs were mounted up.
c The costs were mounting up.
d The costs are mounting up.

→ Now check your answers in the key.

Practise

Rewrite the following sentences so that the meaning stays the same, using the correct form of **mount up**.

a Our bills are increasing at an alarming rate.

_____

b Fuel costs were really starting to increase.

_____

c The legal fees increased and she was no longer able to pay.

_____

d As the debt increases, so too do the interest payments.

_____

e The paperwork soon increases if you don't deal with it at once.

_____

f Her unpaid fines have increased and she now faces prosecution.

_____

g The bank said the losses had begun to increase in 1997.

_____

→ Now check your answers in the key.

58 open up; open something up

FIRST MEANING

Check

Use the sentences in the Study box to help you do these exercises.

MEANING

If an opportunity, a market, etc. **opens up** or somebody or something **opens it up**, does it:

a become more successful?
b become available for the first time?
c become weaker or more difficult?

GRAMMAR

Which of these are grammatically possible?

a New markets have opened up.
b New markets are opening it up.
c It's a change that will open up new markets.
d New markets were opened up by the changes.

→ Now check your answers in the key.

Practise

1 Complete these sentences using an appropriate form of **open up** or **open something up** and any other words you need.

a The government is _____ 30% of the electricity market to competition.

b These reforms will _____ a range of exciting possibilities.

c Huge new markets have _____ by the Internet.

d The change was designed to _____ the technology to a wider audience.

e Workers need savings to pay their bills until another job _____ .

f The deals could _____ new funding for companies.

g New opportunities are _____ in Asia.

2 Write three sentences using a form of **open something up**, including a subject from the list on the left and an object from the list on the right, and any other words you choose:

a the Internet
b the reforms
c telecom operators

i their networks
ii a wider market
iii new job opportunities

_____

_____

_____

→ Now check your answers in the key.

59 open up; **open up** something
SECOND MEANING

> **Study** Read these sentences carefully.
> ▸ Several restaurants have recently **opened up** in the area.
> ▸ The store has **opened up** a new branch in Oxford.
> ▸ We've rebuilt the factory and plan to **open** it **up** as offices.
> ▸ Several new coffee shops have been **opened up** in the city.

Check

Use the sentences in the Study box to help you do these exercises.

MEANING

Choose the word which best completes the meaning of **open up something**.

close	choose	buy	start

to _____

a business, office, store, etc.

GRAMMAR

Which of these are grammatically possible?

a A new store has opened up.
b A new store has opened it up.
c He has opened up a new store.
d A new store was opened up.

→ Now check your answers in the key.

Practise

1 Fill in the gaps in these sentences with the correct form of **open up** or **open up something**.

a We plan to _____ a new branch next year.

b A new branch of the store has _____ nearby.

c Several software companies are _____ in the area.

d The African company has _____ factories to export to the US.

2 Complete the sentences with an appropriate form of **open up** or **open up something** and one of the phrases from the list below:

in Tokyo	a new store	in 2010	new banks

a How many _____ in the town last year?

b There are plans for a motorbike factory to _____ here
_____ .

c I heard that they _____ new offices
_____ a few years ago.

d Are they going _____ here soon?

→ Now check your answers in the key.

Build your vocabulary

OPPOSITES → CLOSE SOMETHING DOWN, CLOSE DOWN on page 25

60 pay something back (to somebody); pay somebody back

Check

Use the sentences in the Study box to help you do these exercises.

MEANING

If you **pay something** or **somebody back**, what do you do? Choose *one* answer.

a You lend somebody some money.
b You punish somebody for something.
c You return money that you borrowed from somebody.

GRAMMAR

There is a grammatical mistake in **one** of the following. Find it and correct it.

a The loan was paid back.
b The company paid it back.
c The company paid back them.
d They were paid back.

→ Now check your answers in the key.

Practise

1 Rearrange these words to make a correct sentence:
company back debts paid the of $3 million _____

2 Choose the correct form of **pay back** to fill the gaps in these sentences.

a You need to _____ within 24 months.
   pay us back/pay back us/paying us back

b Too many people are borrowing money that they have no hope of _____ .
   paying it back/paying back/pay back

c The bank threatened to put the company out of business if they _____ .
   paid the loan back/didn't pay the loan back/didn't paid the loan back

d If you _____ within six months, no interest is charged.
   paying the money back/paid the money back/pay the money back

→ Now check your answers in the key.

Build your vocabulary

RELATED WORDS   NOUN: **payback** (= the money that you receive back on money that you have invested; the time that it takes to get your money back) (This is countable and uncountable.)
- *I'm waiting to get the maximum **payback** on my investment.*
- *a ten-year **payback***

61 pay up; pay up something

Study Read these sentences carefully.

▸ How do you get your customers to **pay up**?
▸ Insurance companies may refuse to **pay up** for some types of theft.
▸ It's time you **paid up** what you owe.
▸ The rent is **paid up** for the next six months.

Check

Use the sentences in the Study box to help you do these exercises.

MEANING

Using three of the words below, complete this meaning of **pay up**.

lend	fees	money	debt
owe	pay	give out	

to _____ someone the _____
that you _____ them, especially
when you do not want to

GRAMMAR

Which of these are grammatically possible?

a The insurance company has still not paid up.
b The insurance company has still not paid the money up.
c The insurance company has still not paid up the money.
d The money has still not been paid up.

→ Now check your answers in the key.

Practise

1 Complete the following sentences below using a form of **pay up**.

a They have threatened to take him to court if he doesn't _____ .
b Some of our customers are very slow in _____ .
c Under the terms of the agreement you have 30 days to _____ .
d Only a few customers have not yet _____ .

2 What could you say in the following situations? Use a form of **pay up** in your answers and any other words you need:

a Have you settled the bill for the hotel?
Yes, it's all _____
b Was the insurance company happy to pay for the damage?
Yes, they _____ *in full immediately.*
c Has she paid her phone bill yet?
No, and they say they'll cut off the phone if _____

→ Now check your answers in the key.

Build your vocabulary

RELATED WORDS ADJECTIVE: **paid-up**
▸ *How many fully **paid-up** members of the union are there?*
(= how many have paid the fee to join?)

SIMILAR VERBS **Settle up** means to pay money that you owe, but unlike **pay up** does not suggest that you do not want to.
▸ *The loan company will allow you to **settle up** early if you wish.*

62 pencil something or somebody in

Study Read these sentences carefully.

▸ We **pencilled in** May 15th as a possible date for the meeting.
▸ So, about our meeting, shall I **pencil** you **in** for tomorrow morning?
▸ We have already **pencilled** a date **in**, but can easily change it.
▸ The product launch has been **pencilled in** for next June.
▸ He was **pencilled in** to speak at the meeting but he had to cancel.

Check

Use the sentences in the Study box to help you do these exercises.

MEANING

If you **pencil something or somebody in**, what do you do?

a you write down an arrangement to do something or see somebody because it is definite

b you make an arrangement to do something or see somebody but you know you may have to change it

GRAMMAR

Which of these are grammatically possible?

a I pencilled it in.
b The meeting has been pencilled in for next week.
c I'll pencil in you for next Tuesday.
d She has been pencilled in to help.

→ Now check your answers in the key.

Practise

1 Fill the spaces with the correct form of **pencil in** and any other words that you need (e.g. him, her, it, etc.).

a The meeting has been _____ for 10.00 on Friday.

b Is it OK with you if I _____ to have lunch with our visitors on Tuesday?

c August 24 was _____ as a possible date.

2 Look at your diary and write some sentences about arrangements you have made for next week that might have to change. Use a form of **pencil in** in each sentence and any other words that you need.

_____
_____
_____

→ Now check your answers in the key.

Build your vocabulary

OTHER MEANINGS **Pencil in** is also used, especially in newspapers, to talk about things that people think will happen but are not completely sure about:

▸ *Analysts have* **pencilled in** *a growth in the group's pre-tax profits for this year.*
▸ *He is* **pencilling in** *a quarter point rise in interest rates in June.*

63 phase something **out**

> **Study** Read these sentences carefully.
> ▸ Several manufacturers are **phasing out** animal testing.
> ▸ They plan to **phase** the system **out** over four years.
> ▸ The chemicals are dangerous, and the industry is now **phasing** them **out**.
> ▸ Tax relief on company cars will be **phased out** over a couple of years.

Check

Use the sentences in the Study box to help you do these exercises.

MEANING

Use two of the words below to complete the meaning of **phase something out**.

> slowly   quickly   stages
> gradually   parts

to remove or stop using something

_____ or in _____

→ Now check your answers in the key.

GRAMMAR

Two of these sentences contain grammatical errors. Find them and correct them.

a The company phased out the system.
b The company phased out it.
c The company phased it out.
d The system phased out.

Practise

1 Two of these sentences can be rewritten using a form of **phase something out**. Choose these sentences and rewrite them.

a The company plans to gradually stop producing children's clothes.
b We will stop offering discounts immediately.
c The train company plans to get rid of first class seats over the next two years.

_____

_____

2 Complete the following sentences using a form of **phase out** and one of the words or phrases below.

> it   nuclear power   700 jobs in the UK   a completely new product

a You can't _____ !

b The product has not sold well and there are plans to _____ .

c Production will be moved to Indonesia and _____ .

d New ways of producing electricity could be found and _____ .

→ Now check your answers in the key.

Build your vocabulary

RELATED WORDS   NOUN: **phase-out** (This is usually used in the singular)
> ▸ *They are planning the gradual **phase-out** of their older planes.*

OPPOSITES   The opposite of **to phase out** is **to phase in**:
> ▸ *The company is **phasing in** a new bonus system.*

64 pick up

Study Read these sentences carefully.

- Trading has been slow but is now **picking up**.
- We're hoping that business will **pick up** again soon.
- There are encouraging signs that consumer spending is **picking up**.
- Economic growth has **picked up** in the second half of the year.

Check

Use the sentences in the Study box to help you do these exercises.

MEANING

Which of these verbs most closely matches this meaning of **pick up**?

a decrease
b change
c improve
d fall

GRAMMAR

There is a mistake in <u>one</u> of these sentences. Find and correct it.

a Sales are picking up.
b Sales were picked up.
c Sales picked up.
d Sales will pick up soon.

→ Now check your answers in the key.

Practise

1 Look at the information below, showing the profits a company has made in 2004 and 2005. Then complete the sentence using this information and the correct form of **pick up**.

	2004	**2005**
profits	$6.5 million	$7.2 million

In 2004, the company made _____ but in 2005 sales _____
and the company made profits of _____

2 Match the two halves to make complete sentences.

a The business may have to close down
b The economy is starting
c The company's sales performance
d Share prices have improved and

i picked up and made a small profit.
ii if sales don't pick up.
iii busines confidence is picking up.
iv to pick up.

3 Rewrite the words that are <u>underlined</u> using an appropriate form of **pick up**:

a Unless passenger numbers **increase** we will miss our target.

_____

b Business has **got better** since we changed our packaging.

_____

c We're hoping that exports will **improve** next year.

_____

d Sales are **looking better** thanks to our new advertising campaign.

_____

→ Now check your answers in the key.

65 prop something up

Study Read these sentences carefully.
- The government will no longer **prop up** inefficient industries.
- The parent company recently paid $50 million to **prop** the business **up**.
- If businesses fail, why should we use tax-payers' money to **prop** them **up**?
- Should failing airlines be **propped up** by their governments?

Check

Use the sentences in the Study box to help you do these exercises.

MEANING

Choose the best words from the brackets to complete this meaning of **prop something up**:

to support something such as a business that is having **(financial/political)** difficulties, especially by giving it **(advice/money)**

GRAMMAR

Which of these are grammatically possible?
a The government will not prop failing businesses up.
b The government will not prop up failing businesses.
c The government will not prop up them.
d Failing businesses will not be propped up by the government.

→ Now check your answers in the key.

Practise

1 Answer the questions about the short text below.

> A billionaire businessman has been found guilty of serious fraud. He had used $600 million from the staff pension fund to prop up his company which was $3 billion in debt.

a Was the company doing well or badly?
b Where did the money to help the company come from?
c Would the company have survived without this money?

2 Complete the following sentences using a form of **prop up** and one of the words or phrases below.

> them   state industries   sales   failing ones

a They had to offer discounts to _____ .

b Their profitable divisions are _____ .

c They claim that European and US farmers rely on their governments to

_____ .

d _____ are sometimes _____ by taxation.

→ Now check your answers in the key.

Build your vocabulary

SYNONYMS **Shore up** means the same as **prop up** and is used in the same way:
- *They borrowed $50 000 to **shore up** their finances.*

SIMILAR VERBS → BAIL SOMEBODY OR SOMETHING OUT on page 3

66 pull out; pull out of something

Study Read these sentences carefully.

▶ The airline collapsed after its main shareholder **pulled out**.
▶ She had accepted the job, but **pulled out** at the last minute.
▶ Airlines are **pulling out of** unprofitable routes.
▶ If the deal isn't finalized by Friday, they say they'll **pull out of** it.

Check

Use the sentences in the Study box to help you do these exercises.

MEANING

Choose the *two* best answers to this question: If someone **pulls out** or **pulls out of something**, do they:

a decide to produce a new product?
b decide to stop being involved in something?
c decide not to do something that they had agreed to do?

GRAMMAR

Which of these are grammatically possible?

a They pulled out at the last minute.
b They pulled out of it at the last minute.
c They were pulled out at the last minute.
d They pulled it out at the last minute.

→ Now check your answers in the key.

Practise

1 Replace the words that are **underlined** with an appropriate form of **pull out** or **pull out of**:

a One US airline **stopped doing business in** Sweden several years ago.

_____

b If we don't raise the money soon, our partners may decide **not to continue**.

_____

c He was due to give a talk at the book fair, but **withdrew** at the last minute.

_____

d The decision to **end** the deal follows the news of poor sales results.

_____

2 Can you suggest some possible answers to the question?
Why did they pull out of the merger?

Because _____

_____

_____

→ Now check your answers in the key.

Build your vocabulary

SYNONYMS The verb **back out** or **back out of something** means the same and is used in the same way.

▶ We can't **back out of** our existing contracts.

67 put something **in**

Study Read these sentences carefully.

- ▸ The department has **put in** a request for extra funding.
- ▸ Buyers have until next Monday to **put** their bids **in**.
- ▸ He withdrew the offer only three days after he had **put** it **in**.
- ▸ The goods were only sent out two months after the order was **put in**.

Check

Use the sentences in the Study box to help you do these exercises.

MEANING

Choose the best words to complete the *two* explanations of this meaning of **put something in**.

1 When you put in a **request/proposal** or **offer/claim** you officially ask for something.

2 When you put in an offer or **bid/ request** you officially offer something.

GRAMMAR

Which of these are grammatically possible?

- a They put an offer in.
- b They put it in.
- c They put in it.
- d The offer was put in.

→ Now check your answers in the key.

Practise

1 Rewrite the words *in italic* in the following sentences, using the correct form of **put in** and any other words you need.

a Our company intends *to make a bid for the contract.* _____

b There is quite a lot of work involved in *making a patent application.*

_____

d He has *made a claim for expenses.* _____

2 Complete the following dialogues using the correct form of **put in** and the noun in brackets.

a Have they applied for planning permission?

Yes, they _____ *last week. (application)*

b How do we ask for time off work?

You have to _____ *to your line manager. (request)*

c Has anyone shown any interest in buying the business?

Yes, someone _____ *last week. (offer)*

→ Now check your answers in the key.

Build your vocabulary

SIMILAR VERBS **To submit** is a more formal way of saying **put in**:
- ▸ She has **submitted** a request to be transferred to another branch.

OPPOSITES **To withdraw:**
- ▸ He put in an offer for the business, but later **withdrew** it.

68 put something **together**

- Managers are hoping to **put together** a successful business plan.
- They're **putting together** a new management team.
- We're at the final stage of **putting** proposals **together**.
- The deal is worth around $7 million and many people were involved in **putting** it **together**.
- The training video has been **put together** by experienced sales reps.

Check

Use the sentences in the Study box to help you do these exercises.

MEANING

1 If you **put together** a business plan, do you

  a attach some pieces of paper together?
  b write down your ideas and present them to somebody?

2 If you **put together** a team, do you

  a choose the people you want?
  b move their desks closer together?

GRAMMAR

Which of these are grammatically possible?
  a They are putting together a deal.
  b The deal was put together by senior managers.
  c The deal is putting together.
  d We have put the deal together.
  e A team of experts was put together.

→ Now check your answers in the key.

Practise

Complete these sentences, using the correct form of **put together** and a suitable noun from the lists at the end of each sentence:

a Managers have _____ a _____ worth $25 million. (**play/deal/card**)

b We are _____ a _____ of experts to try and solve the problem. (**table/policy/group**)

c We _____ our sales _____ in under three weeks. (**energy/force/strength**)

d Jack was the one who had the idea, found the right place and _____ the _____ (**idea/office/operation**)

e The _____ has been _____ as a training aid. (**video/photo/desk**)

→ Now check your answers in the key.

Build your vocabulary

OTHER MEANINGS To **put something together** can also mean 'to make or repair something by fitting parts together':
- *He took the clock apart and couldn't **put** it **together** again.*

69 put up something

- My company **put up** the money to send me on the course.
- A friend offered to **put up** $3 000 if I could find three other backers.
- The school needed $10 000 and a local businessman offered to **put** it **up**.
- She started her own movie company with money **put up** by private investors.

Check

Use the sentences in the Study box to help you do these exercises.

MEANING

Which of the following means the same as to **put up** the money for something?

a To borrow the money for something
b To provide or lend the money for something

GRAMMAR

Which of these is grammatically possible?

a A bank is putting up half the money.
b A bank is putting up it.
c A bank is putting it up.
d Half the money was put up by a bank.

→ Now check your answers in the key.

Practise

1 Match the two halves of these dialogues.

a Do you think the project will go ahead?
b What was Mr. Steel's involvement in the business venture?
c Why was the project cancelled?
d How do you become a limited partner in the business?

i He put up the initial financing.
ii Nobody was willing to put up the money to fund it.
iii You need to put up a minimum of $9 000.
iv It depends on whether we can find someone to put up the money.

2 Complete these sentences using a suitable form of **put up**, the words in brackets and any other words you need.

a If they want to start their own company, they _____ (the cash).

b They agreed to pay half the sum if another organization_____ (half).

c Cigarette companies have been asked _____ for more research on the risks of smoking. (the funding).

→ Now check your answers in the key.

Build your vocabulary

IDIOMS The phrase **put up or shut up** is used for telling somebody that they should either really do what they are talking about or stop talking about it:

- *He was told to **put up or shut up** if he wanted to buy the company.*

OTHER MEANINGS If you **put** something **up for sale**, you offer it for people to buy:

- *The business was **put up for sale** by Deutsche Bank.*

70 report back

- **Report back** after you've talked to her.
- I **reported back on** the meeting to my colleagues.
- He **reported back** that everything was in order.
- She will be **reporting back to** her boss on our progress.

Check

Use the sentences in the Study box to help you do these exercises.

MEANING

Choose the best word to complete the meaning of **report back**.

an article	information	advice
an essay		

to give someone _____
about something they have asked you
to find out

GRAMMAR

Which of these are grammatically possible?

a We reported back on our findings.
b We reported it back on our findings.
c We reported back to our findings.
d We reported back.
e We reported back to the manager.

→ Now check your answers in the key.

Practise

1 Fill the gap in each sentence with the correct form of **report back** and a word from the list below. You may need to use some of them more than once.

with	on	to	from	by	that

a We were asked to _____ our results.

b He _____ everything was progressing well.

c I need to _____ my line manager.

d I'll _____ the meeting.

e After the conference, she _____ her colleagues.

2 You have received this email from your line manager. Write a sentence using **report back**, saying what you have to do.

> Hi. There is a meeting I would like you to attend on March 9 at 2.30 p.m. in Conference Room 2. I can't go but could you come and tell me afterwards what was discussed. Many thanks. James

_____
_____

3 Using the email above as a model, write a similar email to a colleague asking them to tell you about a meeting, a conference, an interview, or some other event that you cannot attend. Use a form of **report back** in your email.

Hi _____
_____
_____
_____

→ Now check your answers in the key.

71 report to somebody

- She **reports to** the marketing director.
- Ms James runs the marketing department and all publicity officers **report to** her.
- Five people **reported** directly **to** the area manager.
- He joins the company as a training assistant, **reporting to** John Thompson.

Check

Use the sentences in the Study box to help you do these exercises.

MEANING

Use three of the words below to complete the meaning of **report to**:

> working   tell   work
> department   responsible

If you **report to** somebody in a company or an organization, they are

_____ for your _____

and _____ you what to do.

→ Now check your answers in the key.

GRAMMAR

Which of the following are grammatically possible?

a He reports to the head of IT.
b He reports to him.
c He reports directly the head of IT.
d He reports to him directly.
e He was reported to the head of IT.

Practise

Look at the diagram of the company's structure, then write more sentences about who **reports to** who.

a Liz Jacobs and Pete Murphy report to Bob Eyre.

b *The IT manager* _____

_____

c _____

_____

d _____

_____

e _____

f *Jack Daniels has just joined as IT assistant* _____

→ Now check your answers in the key.

Ann Smith (managing director)

Tim Jones (assistant managing director)

Bob Eyre (sales manager)

Joan Carr (IT manager)

Brian Tate (production manager)

Liz Jacobs (sales team)

Pete Murphy (sales team)

Jack Daniels (IT assistant)

Tim Pope (production assistant)

Build your vocabulary

RELATED WORDS   A person who **reports to** you is called a **report**:
- *How many **reports** do you have?*
- *I like to have weekly meetings with my **direct reports**.*

72 rip somebody off

Study Read these sentences carefully.

- The bank has been accused of **ripping off** customers.
- By charging so much for tickets, football clubs are **ripping** fans **off**.
- Our company provides reliable tradesmen who won't **rip** you **off**.
- The law protects tenants from being **ripped off** by landlords.

Check

Use the sentences in the Study box to help you do these exercises.

MEANING

Use three of the words or phrases below to complete this meaning of **rip somebody off**.

help	good	a low price	too much	average	poor	cheat

to _____ someone, especially by charging _____ for
something or selling them something of _____ quality

GRAMMAR

Which of these are grammatically possible?

a They are ripping their customers off.
b They are ripping off their customers.
c They are ripping them off.

d They are ripping off them.
e Their customers are being ripped off.

→ Now check your answers in the key.

Practise

1 Complete the following sentence using a form of **rip off** and any other words you need (e.g. her, him, them, etc.)

a She accused the store of

_____

b Many small businesses think that banks

_____

c It is a fair price. We weren't

_____

d They think you've

_____

2 Respond to these comments using a form of **rip off** and any other words you need.

a They charged me $12 for a small sandwich!

You _____

b Did he tell you how much they charged him for the repair?

Yes, they _____

_____

c The tickets were expensive and the concert was terrible!

We _____

_____

→ Now check your answers in the key.

Build your vocabulary

RELATED WORDS   NOUN: **a rip-off** (This is usually a singular noun)
- *They're charging $100 for a part that cost them $5 – what **a rip-off**!*

OPPOSITES   A **bargain** (noun) :
- *I only paid $75 for the DVD player – what a **bargain**!*

73 roll something out

- The airline will **roll out** its new passenger jet in November.
- They are able to **roll** new products **out** very quickly.
- They will introduce the clothing into 84 stores, before **rolling** it **out** across the chain.
- The system will be launched in New York and then **rolled out** across the US.

Check

Use the sentences in the Study box to help you do these exercises.

MEANING

Choose the correct meaning of **roll something out**.

a to start to develop a new product, service or technology

b to make a new product, service or technology available

GRAMMAR

Which of these is grammatically possible?

a They rolled out a new product.
b They rolled a new product out.
c They rolled out it.
d They rolled it out.
e The new product was rolled out.

→ Now check your answers in the key.

Practise

1 There is *one* error in each of these sentences. Find it and correct it.

a The company roll out its new product last month.
b The new version is still being tested, but we hope to roll it by the end of the year.
c The car company rolled up a $15 million ad campaign over the weekend.

2 Rewrite the following sentences, replacing the words **underlined** with the correct form of **roll out**.

a The service will be **be introduced** commercially all across Japan.

b Before **launching** a new product nationally, the company conducts detailed tests.

c We plan to try out the system here and then **make it available** to other regions next year.

d The group **offered** its new car **to the public** on Thursday.

→ Now check your answers in the key.

Build your vocabulary

RELATED WORDS   NOUN: **roll-out** (This is a countable noun)
- *We have been forced to delay the **roll-out** of our new service across the UK.*

SIMILAR VERBS   **Roll out** can also be used without an object:
- *The new phones will start to **roll out** at the end of the year.*

74 round something up (to something)

Study Read these sentences carefully.
- They **rounded up** the price to $750.
- We usually **round** figures **up** in fives or tens.
- The total is $397.83 but shall we **round** it **up** to an even $400?
- Totals should be **rounded up** to the nearest whole number.

50+100+250+100...00=1000
50+100+250+100...00=1000

Check

Use the sentences in the Study box to help you do these exercises.

MEANING

Choose the correct words to complete the meaning of **round something up**.

to make a number **(less/more)** complicated, especially by **(increasing/decreasing)** it to the next **(highest/lowest)** whole number

GRAMMAR

Which of these are grammatically possible?

a I rounded up the figures.
b I rounded the figures up.
c I rounded them up.
d I rounded up them.
e The figures were rounded up.

→ Now check your answers in the key.

Practise

1 Round these numbers up to the nearest whole number:

a 24.7 _____   b 87.86 _____   c 106.5 _____

2 Read the following text then answer the questions.

> Some people blamed the rise in inflation on the change from national currencies to the euro and felt that stores took this opportunity to increase their prices. They did this by always rounding prices up rather than down. People felt that some goods rose in price more than others during this process and that the rounding up of prices happened most commonly in small food stores, restaurants and cafes.

a What did some people think was responsible for the rise in inflation?

_____

b How did stores increase their prices?

_____

c Where did people feel prices rose the most?

_____

3 Look at the text again and complete these sentences using an appropriate form of **round up**.

a The change in currency resulted in prices being _____ .
b Prices were most often _____ in small shops.
c Some stores took advantage of the change in currency to _____ prices.

→ Now check your answers in the key.

Build your vocabulary

OPPOSITES   To **round** a number **down** means to decrease it to the next lowest whole number.

75 rule something or somebody **out** (**as** something); rule something or somebody **out of** something

- ▸ The finance director did not **rule out** the need for further job cuts.
- ▸ We do not want to take industrial action, but we cannot **rule it out** altogether.
- ▸ The proposed solution **was ruled out** as too expensive.
- ▸ They have **ruled out** the marketing director as the next CEO.
- ▸ His age has **ruled him out** for the top job at the bank.
- ▸ That firm yesterday **ruled** itself **out of** the bidding for the contract.

Check

Use the sentences in the Study box to help you do these exercises.

MEANING

Choose the sentence that best matches this meaning of **rule something or somebody out**.

- a to prepare a clear plan or list
- b to explain something clearly
- c to decide that it is impossible for something to happen

GRAMMAR

Which of these are grammatically possible?

- a They ruled out this possibility.
- b They ruled it out.
- c They ruled out it.
- d This possibility was ruled out.
- e He ruled himself out.
- f He ruled out himself of doing it.

→ Now check your answers in the key.

Practise

1 Add *one* word to complete each of the following sentences.

a The possibility of further meetings has not _____ ruled out.

b Although we wish to avoid further job losses, we cannot rule _____ out.

c He has ruled himself out _____ competing for the top job at the firm.

d BP has already ruled _____ out as a potential buyer.

2 Complete the dialogues using an appropriate form of **rule something, somebody or yourself out** and the noun in brackets, adding any other words that you need.

a Is it still possible that there will be a strike?

   No, the union has _____ of a strike. (possibility)

b Is it likely that the two companies will merge?

   No, both sides are _____ . (merger)

c Will more people be made redundant?

   It is possible, as the company has _____ . (further job losses)

→ Now check your answers in the key.

Build your vocabulary

OPPOSITES   **Rule something or somebody in**
- ▸ *The suggestion of a shared contract was not being **ruled in** or ruled out.*

76 run something by/past somebody

Check

Use the sentences in the Study box to help you do these exercises.

MEANING

Choose the words that best complete the meaning of **run something by somebody**.

to **promise/tell/take** somebody something so that they can give you their **answer/email/opinion**.

GRAMMAR

Which of these are grammatically possible?

a I'd like to run a few ideas by you.
b I'd like to run past a few ideas you.
c I ran a few ideas by him.
d I'd like to run it past you.
e It was run past a few people.

→ Now check your answers in the key.

Practise

1 Complete the sentences using a suitable form of **run by/past** and the word or phrase in brackets.

a I'll have to _____ my line manager before I can give you an answer. **(it)**

b She _____ the sales team to see what they thought. **(the figures)**

c Do you mind if I _____ you concerning the advertising campaign? **(some suggestions)**

d I was nervous about _____ the bank manager. **(my business plan)**

2 Write a suitable answer to each of these questions, using an appropriate form of **run something by/past somebody**.

a Why did you go to see your accountant?

_____

b What do you want to see me about?

_____

c What were you talking to the Marketing Manager about?

_____

→ Now check your answers in the key.

77 run up something

Study Read these sentences carefully.

▶ They have **run up** a bill of $20 million in lawyer's fees.
▶ He had **run up** extremely large debts.
▶ The telephone bill was so huge I couldn't believe we had **run it up** in a month.
▶ Massive budget deficits have been **run up** by the local government.

Check

Use the sentences in the Study box to help you do these exercises.

MEANING

1 Choose the word that best completes this meaning of **run something up**.

give   earn   owe

to do something that causes you to

_____ a lot of money

2 Which of these might you **run up**? Circle the right answers.

a debt   a salary   costs   a deficit   a bill   a cab

GRAMMAR

Which of these are grammatically possible?

a He ran up a huge bill.
b He ran it up in one year.
c He ran up it.
d The bill has been run up by the council.

→ Now check your answers in the key.

Practise

1 Complete these sentences using an appropriate form of **run up**:

a She _____ huge debts last year.

b He had _____ a phone bill of $700.

c Huge losses had been _____ by one rogue trader.

d Most students get jobs to avoid _____ large debts.

2 Discussion. Write some full sentences in answer to these questions:

a Can you think of some ways in which a company might run up large debts?

_____

b What is the largest bill you've ever run up? What was it for? How long did it take you to pay it?

_____

→ Now check your answers in the key.

Build your vocabulary

SYNONYMS   **Accumulate something** has a similar meaning:

▶ *Consumers **are accumulating** debt at a rapid pace.*

It can also be used in a positive way:

▶ *The easiest way to **accumulate** wealth is to run your own business.*

78 sell something off

Check

Use the sentences in the Study box to help you do these exercises.

MEANING

Choose the best explanation of the meaning of **sell something off**.

a to sell a new product
b to sell a product online
c to sell all or part of a business

GRAMMAR

Which of these are grammatically possible?
a He sold off the business.
b The business was sold off.
c He sold off it.
d He sold it off.
e He was selling off it.

→ Now check your answers in the key.

Practise

Complete the sentences by choosing the correct form of **sell off**.

a The business was _____ last year.
   sell off/sell it off/sold off

b The company plans to _____ its IT division.
   sell off/selling off/sold off

c We acquired the company five years ago and _____ last year.
   sold off it/sold it off/sell off it

d We plan to _____
   sell the division off/selling off the division/sold the division off

e Most of the assets have been _____ already.
   selling off/sells off/sold off

→ Now check your answers in the key.

Build your vocabulary

RELATED WORDS   NOUN: **a sell-off** (= the sale by the government of an industry or a service to individual people or private companies) (This is a countable noun.)
▸ *If the **sell-off** of the rail company goes ahead, many jobs will be lost.*

SIMILAR VERBS   If you **auction something off**, you sell it to the person who offers the most money at a public sale.
▸ *Some of the firm's buildings and vehicles have now been **auctioned off**.*

79 set something up

Study Read these sentences carefully.
- ▶ He has **set up** a meeting for tomorrow.
- ▶ My secretary is **setting** all the interviews **up**.
- ▶ If you want to talk to Mr. Jackson, I'll **set** it **up** for you.
- ▶ The arrangements **set up** by the two companies were very different.

Check

Use the sentences in the Study box to help you do these exercises.

MEANING

If you set up a meeting, you…
- a decide to have it
- b put out chairs
- c attend it
- d arrange it

GRAMMAR

There is a grammatical error in **one** of these sentences. Find it and correct it.
- a Helen set up an interview.
- b Helen set an interview up.
- c Helen set it up.
- d Helen set up it.
- e The interview has been set up.

→ Now check your answers in the key.

Practise

Complete the sentences with the correct form of **set up** and one of the words and phrases below:

| it | an interview | a meeting | a talk | the transport arrangements | my appointments |

a If you're interested in the job I'll _____ for you.

b I think we should _____ to discuss this issue before it gets out of control.

c My assistant is responsible for _____ .

d The conference was a great success. Thanks to everyone involved in

_____ .

e You have to get to London by 10? I'll _____ .

f We've _____ for anyone interested in starting their own business.

→ Now check your answers in the key.

Build your vocabulary

OTHER MEANINGS You may already know **set something up, set up** meaning 'to create or start a company, a business or an organization':
- ▶ *She left the company to **set up** her own business.*
- ▶ *He took out a bank loan and **set up** in business on his own.*

Set something up can also mean 'to start a process or a series of events':
- ▶ *The slump on Wall Street **set up** a chain reaction in stock markets around the world.*

80 shake something or somebody up

- The new manager **shook up** the sales team and brought in four new people.
- We are hoping that the new board will **shake** the business **up** a bit.
- The company's entry into the market should **shake** it **up**.
- The group's European operation has been **shaken up**.

Check

Use the sentences in the Study box to help you do these exercises.

MEANING

Which of these best describes what you do if you **shake up** a business or an organization?

a you open new offices
b you start to lose money
c you make changes in order to improve it

GRAMMAR

Two of these sentences have grammatical errors in them. Find them and correct them.

a The new manager should shake up it.
b The new manager should shake the business up.
c The new manager should shake it up the business.
d The new manager should shake it up.
e The business was shaken up by the new manager.

→ Now check your answers in the key.

Practise

1 Match the two halves to make complete sentences.

a The whole industry needs
b The sales department isn't doing well so
c The new CEO has already
d The board brought me in to
e Increased competition will

i shake up the market.
ii there are plans to shake it up.
iii shake things up.
iv shaken us up.
v shaking up.

2 Think about changes that could be made to improve an organization that you know and write *two* sentences about it using **shake something or somebody up**.

_____

_____

_____

→ Now check your answers in the key.

Build your vocabulary

RELATED WORDS NOUN: **shake-up.** This noun is usually used in the singular.

- *There are plans for a major **shake-up** of the business.*
- *They are predicting a big **shake-up** in the telecoms industry.*
- *Shareholders demanded a management **shake-up**.*

81 shop around; shop around something

Study Read these sentences carefully.
- Customers will continue to **shop around** for the lowest prices.
- We **shopped around** to find a good lawyer.
- Prices of PCs vary considerably so you should **shop around**.
- It's worth **shopping around** the travel agents to find the best deals.

Check

Use the sentences in the Study box to help you do these exercises.

MEANING

Which *one* of these best matches
the meaning of **shop around**?

a to visit lots of stores and buy
   lots of things
b to buy lots of things from one store
c to compare goods in different stores
   before deciding which to buy

GRAMMAR

Which of these are grammatically possible?

a It is a good idea to shop around.
b It is a good idea to shop it around.
c We shopped around.
d We were shopped around.

→ Now check your answers in the key.

Practise

1 Fill in *one* word to complete each of these sentences.

a She always _____ around before she makes a purchase.

b I'm shopping around _____ find the lowest prices.

c It is worth shopping around _____ the best insurance deal.

d It's a good idea to shop around to _____ the bank that offers
   the best service.

e If you're buying a DVD player, shop around for the _____ price.

2 Complete these sentences with the correct form of **shop around**.

a Parents are _____ to find good schools.

b It's best to _____ before committing yourself to one company.

c If you don't like the price you can _____ .

d It is much easier to strike a bargain when you have _____ .

3 Rewrite these advertisements so that the meaning stays the same, using a
   form of **shop around**.

> a CUSTOMERS SHOULD LOOK FOR THE BEST INSURANCE DEAL.

_____

> b BUYING A NEW CAR? DON'T LOOK AT LOTS OF OTHER PLACES. OUR PRICES ARE LOWEST!

_____

→ Now check your answers in the key.

82 sign up; sign somebody up

- Stores try to encourage customers to **sign up for** their store cards.
- She has **signed up with** an employment agency.
- Customers **signing up to** the new service will be offered a choice of three handsets.
- Over two hundred companies have **signed up** to take part in the scheme.
- The main telephone providers are racing against each other to **sign up** customers.
- Within a week, they had **signed** 200 students **up for** the scheme.
- We try to give customers as much information as possible when we **sign** them **up**.
- He has been **signed up** as their new sales director.

Check

Use the sentences in the Study box to help you do these exercises.

MEANING

When somebody **signs up**, they sign their name on a document. What might somebody **sign up** for? Choose all the correct possibilities.

a to agree to use and pay for a service
b to agree to become a member of something
c to agree to receive goods and pay for them
d to agree to leave your job

GRAMMAR

Which of these are grammatically possible?

a He signed up for something.
b He signed up with a company.
c The company signed customers up.
d The company signed him up.
e The company signed up him.

You *sign up* **with** a company or an organization **for** a particular service.
You *sign up* **to** an agreement, a deal or, less often, a service.

→ Now check your answers in the key.

Practise

1 Complete the following sentences using an appropriate form of **sign up** and any other words you need. You will need a preposition in some sentences.

a He went for an interview with the company, and they are very keen to

_____ .

b I wanted to learn more about accounting, so I _____ an accountancy training course.

c The company _____ over 2 000 customers since May.

d Sandra wanted to find a job so she _____ a temping agency.

e They are hoping that a lot of people will want _____ the free email service.

2 Have you ever **signed up** to do any of these things?

a to buy an insurance policy.
b to go on a training course.
c to become a member of a club or society
d to take part in an event for charity

→ Now check your answers in the key.

83 smarten something or somebody up

- ▶ The company has spent over $3 million on **smartening up** its retail outlets.
- ▶ Shop staff were told to **smarten** the displays **up**.
- ▶ They painted the office to **smarten** it **up**.
- ▶ The reception area has been **smartened up** with new carpets and furniture.
- ▶ She was told to **smarten** herself **up** as she was dealing with the public.

Check

Use the sentences in the Study box to help you do these exercises.

MEANING

Choose *all* the correct possibilities from the words below to complete the meaning of **smarten up**.

| more attractive | cleaner | more untidy |
| neater | more expensive | darker |

If you smarten a place or a person up, you make it/them look _____

GRAMMAR

Which of these are grammatically possible?

a They smartened up the store.
b They smartened the store up.
c They smartened it up.
d They smartened up it.
e He smartened himself up.
f He smartened up himself.

→ Now check your answers in the key.

Practise

1 There is *one* mistake in each of the following sentences. Find it and correct it.

a She will have to smarten herself if she wants to be promoted.
b Our head office used to look old-fashioned and dirty, but we've smartened up now.
c They have asked all their staff to smarten their up appearance.

2 Complete the dialogues using an appropriate form of **smarten up** and any other words you need.

a The hotel looks a bit dull and old-fashioned now.
   Yes, we definitely need to _____

b Do you think we need to change the packaging of our products?
   It could easily be _____

c This used to be such a lovely town.
   A lot of money needs to be spent on _____ *to attract tourists again.*

→ Now check your answers in the key.

Build your vocabulary

SIMILAR VERBS **Smarten up** can sometimes be used without an object:
   ▶ *A memo was sent round the office ordering staff to **smarten up**.*

   → CLEAN SOMETHING UP on page 24

84 start up; start something up

Study Read these sentences carefully.

▸ When I **started up** in business I needed a lot of help.
▸ How many businesses **started up** in this area last year?
▸ He is planning to **start up** a new company.
▸ Although it's a family firm, it was my wife who **started** it **up**.
▸ The company was **started up** in 2004.

Check

Use the sentences in the Study box to help you do these exercises.

MEANING

If a business **starts up** or somebody **starts** one **up**, does it:

a begin to grow?
b begin to sell more expensive goods?
c begin to trade?

GRAMMAR

Which of these are grammatically possible?

a She started up a business.
b She started it up.
c She started up it.
d The business was started up by her father.
e The business started itself up.

→ Now check your answers in the key.

Practise

Complete the sentences using a form of the verb **start up** and one of the words or phrases from the list below.

one   a new business of their own   its second UK base   on the Web   your own company
on her own   a free newspaper   September

a They used the loan to _____ .

b A young journalist has _____ in the town.

c There are several organizations that can offer you advice on how to

_____ .

d I've always wanted my own company and now I'm _____ .

e She resigned her position as managing director and _____ .

f Initially, we'll lose money when we _____ .

g Many new insurance ventures have _____ since _____ .

h The airline is _____ at Bournemouth.

→ Now check your answers by on p. 000.

Build your vocabulary

RELATED WORDS   ADJECTIVE: **start-up** (= connected with beginning a new business)
▸ *The **start-up** costs came to around $2 million.*

NOUN: **start-up** (This is a countable noun.)
▸ *The fund invests in Internet **start-ups**.*

85 step down (as/from something)

▶ She is **stepping down** after four years in the job.
▶ He has decided to **step down** as director of the company.
▶ No one knows who will replace the Governor of the Bank of England when he **steps down** in March.
▶ Although she is **stepping down** from the committee, she will still be involved with the organization.

Check

Use the sentences in the Study box to help you do these exercises.

MEANING

Which of these is closest in meaning to **step down**?

a to change jobs
b to start a new job
c to leave an important job or position

GRAMMAR

Which of these are grammatically possible?

a She stepped down.
b She stepped down from the job.
c She stepped herself down.
d She is stepping down.
e She is stepping down the job.

→ Now check your answers in the key.

Practise

1 Complete the following sentences using one of these prepositions: **from/as**

a Ms. Black will step down _____ head of the department in January.

b Mr. Clarke stepped down _____ chairman last year.

c She is stepping down _____ the committee due to other work commitments.

2 Complete the following sentences with an appropriate form of **step down**.

a He has finally _____ after fifteen years as the company's CEO.

b She was forced to _____ last May.

c He has announced that he is _____ as chairman next month.

d I have heard that Ms Hudd has _____ from the management committee.

e He is under pressure from shareholders to _____ .

→ Now check your answers in the key.

Build your vocabulary

SYNONYMS   **Step aside**, **stand down** and **stand aside** mean the same as **step down**:
▶ *Mr Brown has announced that he is **standing down** as chairman next month.*
▶ *I think it's time for me to **step aside** and let someone younger take over the job.*

SIMILAR VERBS   **Resign** has a similar meaning but means 'to tell someone officially that you are leaving your job':
▶ *Mr Brown has **resigned** as chairman.*

86 stock up (on/with something)

Study Read these sentences carefully.
- ▸ Supermarkets **stocked up** on ice cream because of the hot weather.
- ▸ Stores are **stocking up** for the huge demand that is expected.
- ▸ I've already **stocked up** with plenty of dollars for my trip.
- ▸ Drug wholesalers have been **stocking up** ahead of expected price increases.

Check

Use the sentences in the Study box to help you do these exercises.

MEANING

Which of these best matches this meaning of **stock up**?

a to buy a lot of something so you can use or sell it later
b to display the things that you are selling

GRAMMAR

Which of these are grammatically possible?

a Stores are stocking up.
b Stores are stocking themselves up.
c Stores are stocking up on the new toys.
d Stores are stocking up the new toys.
e Stores are stocking up with toys.

→ Now check your answers in the key.

Practise

1 There is **one** mistake in each of the following sentences. Can you find it and correct it?

a We need to stock up for flowers to meet the huge demand.
b The book was very popular so bookstores stocked it up.
c He is going to use the money to stock up of new products.

2 Complete the following sentences with the correct form of **stock up** and one of the words or phrases in the list.

| day | warm clothes | inventory | cold drinks | the holiday season |

a Shoppers are already _____ on _____ for the winter.
b The weather was very hot so the supermarkets _____ on
_____ .
c Stores are starting to _____ for _____ .
d Some shops _____ every _____ .
e This store never _____ on _____
unless they know it will definitely sell.

→ Now check your answers in the key.

Build your vocabulary

OTHER MEANINGS **Stock up** can also be used with an object to mean 'to fill something with goods':
- ▸ I **stocked up** the freezer for the family before I went to the conference.

It is often used in the form **be stocked up**:
- ▸ The stationery cupboard **was stocked up** with paper and pens.

87 take off

Study Read these sentences carefully.

- ▶ It was several years before the business really **took off**.
- ▶ His career began to **take off** in the 1990s.
- ▶ Sales on the Internet have **taken off** in recent years
- ▶ Our new service is not **taking off** as we had hoped.

Check

Use the sentences in the Study box to help you do these exercises.

MEANING

Choose the correct *two* words to complete this meaning of **take off**.

> correct successful popular
> unimportant

When something takes off it becomes

very _____ or _____

GRAMMAR

Which of these are grammatically possible?

- **a** The business took off.
- **b** It took off.
- **c** He took off the business.
- **d** The business was taking off.
- **e** The business was taken off.

→ Now check your answers in the key.

Practise

1 There is <u>one</u> error in each of the following sentences. Find it and correct it.

- **a** It started as a small company, but was really taken off now.
- **b** His career really taking off when he moved to the States.
- **c** Job-sharing started to take on in the 1990s.

2 Replace the **<u>underlined</u>** words with an appropriate form of **take off**.

- **a** Sales have **increased dramatically** over the last six months.

  _____

- **b** The idea **became popular** in America first.

  _____

- **c** He expects the business to **grow quickly** over the next five to ten years.

  _____

- **d** This type of insurance policy never really **became popular** in Britain.

  _____

- **e** There is no sign of our new product **making a lot of money** for a while.

  _____

→ Now check your answers in the key.

Build your vocabulary

RELATED WORDS NOUN: **take-off** (This is a countable and an uncountable noun.)
- ▶ *The economy is poised for **take-off**.*
- ▶ *There has been a slow **take-off** for video phones.*

88 take somebody on

Study Read these sentences carefully.

▶ The economy is improving and many firms are **taking on** new staff.
▶ They're **taking** two more people **on** to help with the orders.
▶ It can be difficult to persuade companies to **take** you **on** once you are over 50.
▶ I was **taken on as** a management trainee.

Check

Use the sentences in the Study box to help you do these exercises.

MEANING

Which of these sentences gives a correct explanation of this meaning of **take somebody on**?

a to refuse to give somebody a job
b to have a job
c to give somebody a job

GRAMMAR

Which of these are grammatically possible?

a They took on more staff.
b They took them on.
c They took on them.
d More staff were taken on.
e They took more staff on.

→ Now check your answers by on p. 000.

Practise

1 Match the two halves to make complete sentences.

a He took on an assistant
b The company is taking on extra staff
c We would not have taken him on
d Since September they have taken on

i 40 new staff.
ii if we had known he was not qualified.
iii because he had too much work.
iv to cope with increased demand.

2 Rewrite these sentences so that the meaning stays the same, using an appropriate form of **take on** and any other words you need.

a The company usually gives jobs to quite a lot of students during the summer.
The company _____

b Firms are now much more willing to give jobs to disabled people.
Firms _____

c I applied for a job with Wilkinson Brothers, but they didn't give me one.
I applied _____

d After a three month trial period, she was given a job as an area manager.
After _____

→ Now check your answers in the key.

Build your vocabulary

SYNONYMS **Employ** and **recruit** mean the same as **take on**. **Hire** is also used, especially in American English.

▶ They have **employed** *fifty new workers.*
▶ The business **recruits** *a number of new graduates every year.*
▶ She is responsible for **hiring** *new staff.*

OPPOSITES → LAY SOMEBODY OFF on page 51

89 take somebody or something on

- ▸ The price will have to be right if this car is to **take on** its rivals.
- ▸ He felt strongly enough about it to **take** the company **on** in court.
- ▸ While he was still young, he **took on** the big corporations and won.
- ▸ These corporations are so powerful that smaller firms cannot **take** them **on**.

Check

Use the sentences in the Study box to help you do these exercises.

MEANING

Use the words below to complete this meaning of **take somebody or something on**.

more	less	do business	compete	defeat	fight

to _____ with someone or _____ against them, especially

somebody who is _____ powerful than you

GRAMMAR

Which of these are grammatically possible?

a They took their rivals on.   **c** They took them on.
b They took on their rivals.   **d** They took on them.

→ Now check your answers in the key.

Practise

1 Complete each of these sentences with an appropriate form of **take somebody on**
and one of the words or phrases below:

her former employers	the competition	the market leader
them	the traditional chain stores	

a No other software company has yet _____ .

b The industry is dominated by the big banks, but now we _____ .

c New bargain superstores are opening up and _____ .

d The company has a lot of faith in this new cleaning product, and believes that it can

_____ .

e She decided to _____ and sue them for unfair dismissal.

2 Read these headlines and say what you think the articles are about.

a   How we took on the big airlines.

_____

b   The government promises to take on big polluters.

_____

→ Now check your answers in the key.

90 take something on

Study

Read these sentences carefully.
- ▶ People who are self-employed often **take on** too much work.
- ▶ She **took on** more responsibilities when she was promoted.
- ▶ He's **taken** a lot of extra work **on** recently.
- ▶ It's a difficult job and no-one seems to want to **take it on**.
- ▶ The report looks at the amount of consultancy work **taken on** by senior managers.

Check

Use the sentences in the Study box to help you do these exercises.

MEANING

If you **take on** some work, do you

a refuse to do it?
b agree to do it?
c continue doing it?

GRAMMAR

Which of these are grammatically possible?

a I took on the work.
b I took the work on.
c I took on it.
d Extra work was taken on.

→ Now check your answers in the key.

Practise

1 Complete each of these sentences with the correct form of **take on** and one of the words or phrases below:

> this task   too much work   such a big project   part-time work
> an extra day's work   his case   sales and marketing

a My doctor advised me not to _____ .

b She had to deal with complaints herself because no-one else was willing to

_____ .

c Whoever _____

should be able to work under pressure.

d Our firm has never _____ before.

e She is _____ to help pay the bills.

f He couldn't find a solicitor willing to _____ .

g There has been an increase in the amount of _____
by students.

2 Think about some work, responsibilities or jobs that you have taken on recently. Write two or three sentences about this, using a form of the verb **take on** in each.

_____

_____

_____

→ Now check your answers in the key.

91 take something over

Study Read these sentences carefully.

▶ They have made an informal offer to **take over** the airline.
▶ The government **took** the electricity company **over** as part of its nationalization plan.
▶ The company was making huge losses when we **took** it **over**.
▶ Analysts think that the electronics group will **be taken over** by a rival.

Check

Use the sentences in the Study box to help you do these exercises.

MEANING

Choose the best meaning of this use of **take over**:

a to sell a company
b to invest in a company
c to gain control of a company
d to take money from a company

GRAMMAR

There is a grammatical mistake in <u>one</u> of these sentences. Find it and correct it.

a They took over the company.
b They took the company over.
c They will over take the company.
d The company has been taken over.
e We are going to take it over.

→ Now check your answers in the key.

Practise

1 Match the two halves to make complete sentences.

a The telecoms company was
b A record production company
c The giant textile group has
d Only one electricity company can

i took the retail stores over.
ii taken over its nearest rival.
iii take over a bigger share of the power market.
iv taken over by a private operator.

2 Complete each of these sentences with the correct form of **take over**.

a Several companies are bidding to _____ the food retailer.

b Did you know that an American group is _____ the local car maker?

c The football club will be _____ by the finance company at the end of this month.

d Analysts believe that the group could be _____ at less than 190¢ a share.

e The business was already highly profitable when Blake Ltd _____ it

_____ .

→ Now check your answers in the key.

Build your vocabulary

RELATED WORDS   NOUN: **a takeover** (This is a countable and an uncountable noun.)
▶ *More than 400 jobs were lost as a result of **the takeover**.*
▶ *Sony was the target of **a takeover bid** by CBS records.*

92 take over (from somebody) (as something); take something over (from somebody)

Study Read these sentences carefully.

- ▶ Who will **take over** as manager when Jack retires?
- ▶ Sales were falling until the Marketing Manager **took over**.
- ▶ Mrs Waters will **take over** from the current Chairman.
- ▶ He **took** the business **over** from his father in 2003.
- ▶ The department was losing money so she decided to **take** it **over** and run it herself.
- ▶ The top job at the firm is being **taken over** by the present sales director.

Check

Use the sentences in the Study box to help you do these exercises.

MEANING

Choose the best meaning of this use of **take over**:

- a to join somebody in doing a job
- b to give a job to another person
- c to take responsibility for something after somebody else

GRAMMAR

Which of these are grammatically possible?

- a He took over the job.
- b He took it over.
- c He took over as the job.
- d He took over from the manager.

→ Now check your answers in the key.

Practise

1 There is *one* error in each of the following sentences. Find it and correct it.

- a Ms Camus take over the post next week.
- b The business has started to make a profit since he took over CEO last March.
- c The new boss only took over from control a few weeks ago.
- d I'm sorry to hear you're leaving. We'll need somebody special to take you over.

2 Complete the following sentences using a form of **take over** and a preposition if necessary.

- a Who is going _____ Sam when she leaves?

- b Who is going _____ Sam's job when she leaves?

- c Amy _____ sales manager when Mike left.

- d He has made a lot of money since _____ the family business.

- e The new CEO _____ the running of the company next week.

→ Now check your answers in the key.

Build your vocabulary

OTHER MEANINGS **Take over** is also used in a similar way to mean to do somebody's job for them for a short time:

- ▶ *I've just got to pop out – can you **take over** the Help Desk for half an hour?*
- ▶ *You've been on the Help Desk for hours! Would you like me to **take over**?*

93 tie something up

FIRST MEANING

Study Read these sentences carefully.

▸ Both companies are keen to **tie up** a deal.
▸ We have reached an agreement now — it's just a question of **tying up** a few things.
▸ Talks about a deal have been going on and we hope to **tie** it **up** soon.
▸ There will be a meeting tomorrow to allow the final details to be **tied up**.

Check

Use the sentences in the Study box to help you do these exercises.

MEANING

Which of these best matches this meaning of **tie something up**?

a to start talking about arrangements for something
b to have a meeting with someone to discuss a deal
c to finish arranging the details of something

GRAMMAR

Which of these are grammatically correct?

a He tied up the deal.
b He tied up it.
c He tied it up.
d He tied the deal up.
e The deal was tied up.
f The deal tied up.

→ Now check your answers in the key.

Practise

1 Read the following newspaper article and **underline** two verbs that could be replaced with a form of **tie up**.

TALKS NEARING AN END
Talks have been continuing this week over the proposed merger of a British steel company with a Japanese one. Managers are hoping that the deal will be completed in the next few weeks and that the financial arrangements can be sorted out.

2 Replace the words that are **underlined** with a suitable form of **tie up**:

a We hope to **agree upon** the details

during the course of these negotiations.

_____

b The two companies have **organized** a merger which will take place next year.

_____

c If all goes to plan, we should be able to **arrange** the deal in a couple of weeks.

_____

d We've done most of the work now. We're just **finalizing** the last details.

_____

→ Now check your answers in the key.

Build your vocabulary

IDIOMS   **tie up loose ends**

▸ This is a common idiom meaning 'to deal with the last details or small jobs':
▸ *I'm just **tying up loose ends** before I go off on leave.*

94 tie something **up** (**in** something)

SECOND MEANING

> **Study** Read these sentences carefully.
> ▸ We wouldn't want to **tie up** cash for as long as that.
> ▸ Young people generally don't like **tying** money **up** in a pension fund.
> ▸ You could invest the money in a pension fund but may not want to **tie** it **up** for so long.
> ▸ Most of our capital **is tied up** in property.

Check

Use the sentences in the Study box to help you do these exercises.

MEANING

Choose the verb that best fills the gap to complete this meaning of **tie something up**.

to **earn/invest/spend/lose** money in such a way that it cannot be used for anything else

GRAMMAR

Which of these are grammatically correct?

a The investment will tie up a lot of money.
b A lot of money was tied up in the investment.
c The investment will tie a lot of money up.
d The investment will tie it.

→ Now check your answers in the key.

Practise

1 Circle the correct form of **tie something up** in each sentence.

a Too many resources will be **tying up/tied up** in the project.
b The deal will **tie up/ties up** a lot of money for a long time.
c We need to reduce the cash that is **tie up/tied up** in inventory.

2 Complete the answers to the following questions using a form of **tie something up**, the word or phrase in brackets and any other words you need.

a Why don't you want to invest in the fund?
  All my money ＿＿＿＿＿＿＿＿＿＿＿＿＿＿＿＿＿＿＿＿ . **(property)**

b Why doesn't the company have more money available?
  Its assets ＿＿＿＿＿＿＿＿＿＿＿＿＿＿＿＿＿＿＿ . **(raw materials)**

c Why haven't you got any money at the moment?
  I have ＿＿＿＿＿＿＿＿ *all my capital* ＿＿＿＿＿＿＿＿＿ . **(my business)**

d They don't seem to have much available cash.
  They might be ＿＿＿＿＿＿＿＿＿＿＿＿＿＿＿*in inventory.* **(too much cash)**

→ Now check your answers in the key.

Build your vocabulary

SIMILAR VERBS **Tie somebody up** has a similar meaning: 'to keep somebody so busy that they have no time for other things'.
  ▸ *I'm **tied up** in a meeting until three.*

OPPOSITES If you **free up** money you make it available.

95 turn something **around**; turn around

Study Read these sentences carefully.
- ▸ He gave himself two years to **turn** the company **around**.
- ▸ The job cuts are intended to **turn around** the performance of the supermarket quickly.
- ▸ The company buys failing businesses and tries to **turn** them **around**.
- ▸ How can this situation **be turned around**?
- ▸ The company has **turned around** in the last three years, adding more than 1.5 million customers and increasing profits.

Check

Use the sentences in the Study box to help you do these exercises.

MEANING

If someone turns a business around or it turns around, what happens?

a the business goes bankrupt
b the business is sold
c the business starts to improve
d employees leave

GRAMMAR

Which of these are grammatically possible?

a He turned the business around.
b He turned around the business.
c He turned around it.
d The business was turned around.
e The business turned around.
f He turned it around.

→ Now check your answers in the key.

Practise

Choose a a subject or object from the list below and complete the sentences using an appropriate form of **turn around** in each sentence .

the business   its falling European car sales   a struggling company
failing businesses   the job market

a He was hired for his experience in _____ .

b The car maker is struggling to _____ .

c _____ by its new owners.

d _____ hasn't _____ yet, and unemployment is still rising.

e You can no longer _____ by just cutting jobs and making staff redundant.

→ Now check your answers in the key.

Build your vocabulary

RELATED WORDS   NOUN: **a turnaround** (also **turnround** in British English). This is usually used as a singular noun.
  ▸ *The predicted economic **turnaround** failed to happen.*

SIMILAR VERBS   In British English you can use **turn something round** instead of **turn something around**:
  ▸ *He managed to **turn** the business **round** in less than two years.*

96 turn down

95 turn something around · turn...

> **Study** Read these sentences carefully.
> - When the economy **turns down**, small businesses tend to suffer more.
> - Sales had been good, but began to **turn down** towards the end of last year.
> - A company's weaknesses are often exposed when the market **turns down**, as it did in 1992.

Check

Use the sentences in the Study box to help you do these exercises.

MEANING

Choose the correct words to complete the meanings of **turn down**.

a If the economy **turns down**, it becomes **stronger/weaker** and **more/less** successful.

b If sales **turn down**, they **increase/decrease**.

GRAMMAR

Which of these are grammatically possible?

a The economy turned down.
b It turned itself down.
c This turned the economy down.
d The economy was turned down.
e The economy is turning down.

→ Now check your answers in the key.

Practise

1 Complete the sentences with one of the words below and the correct form of **turn down**.

> economy   market   profits

a Recently, sales have fallen and _____ have _____ .

b The _____ for this type of product has _____ recently.

c The government now fears that the _____ may be beginning to

_____ .

2 Find three verbs or phrases in the following text that mean the same as **turn down**. Then replace them with an appropriate form of **turn down**.

> Despite some positive signs, most analysts now believe that the economy is beginning to become weaker. Demand in some key markets such as housing has declined, and many businesses have seen their sales and profits decrease over the last six months.

a _____   b _____   c _____

→ Now check your answers in the key.

Build your vocabulary

RELATED WORDS   NOUN: **a downturn** This is usually used as a singular noun.
> - There has been a **downturn** in sales this year.

The opposite is an **upturn**:
> - There has been an **upturn** in demand.

97 turn something out

Study Read these sentences carefully.

▸ The factory **turns out** 900 cars a week.
▸ There are 350 workers building computers, **turning out** 2 000 units per day.
▸ There's still a huge demand for her books and she just keeps **turning** them **out**!
▸ Around sixty new caravans **are turned out** each month.

Check

Use the sentences in the Study box to help you do these exercises.

MEANING

Which of these verbs means the same as **turn something out**?

a get rid of
b lose
c produce

GRAMMAR

Which of these are grammatically possible?

a They turn out 1000 tons of paper every week.
b They turn it out every week.
c They turn out it every week.
d 1000 tons of paper are turned out every week.

→ Now check your answers in the key.

Practise

1 Match the two halves to make complete sentences

a The restaurant always turns out
b The school is famous for turning out
c It can take months to turn out
d They have invested in a new plant so they can turn out
e I've heard that the factory turns out

i 400 000 new cars a year.
ii just a few seconds of screen time.
iii large numbers of business graduates every year.
iv perfectly cooked food.
v even more new products.

2 Rewrite the sentences using an appropriate form of **turn out** and any other words you need:

a The factory makes a variety of medical devices.

_____

b The plant once put together 650 engines per day.

_____

c Analysts are expecting the company to make a ¥5 billion profit this year.

_____

d The operation is currently producing 800 000 barrels a day.

_____

e Most of our revenue lies in making paper for magazines and writing pads.

_____

→ Now check your answers in the key.

98 turn something over to somebody

▶ The team will **turn over** many of its functions to the sales department.
▶ She **turned** the business **over** to her son.
▶ He had the business for a long time and was reluctant to **turn** it **over** to anyone else.
▶ The project was **turned over** to a US company.

Check

Use the sentences in the Study box to help you do these exercises.

MEANING

Choose the best verb to complete the meaning of **turn something over to somebody**.

to *advertise/give/show* power, responsibility or a business to somebody else

GRAMMAR

Which of these are grammatically possible?

a She turned over the business to her partner.
b She turned it over to her partner.
c She turned over it to her partner.
d The business was turned over to her partner.

→ Now check your answers in the key.

Practise

1 Fill in the gaps in the sentences with the correct form of **turn over**.

a He will _____ the management of the project to his assistant next year.

b Control of the business should now be _____ to a professional manager.

c The company is _____ production to contractors.

d How long will it be before she _____ responsibility for the project to someone else in the team?

2 There is **one** error in each of the following sentences. Find it and correct it.

a She turned up a share of her company's stock to her children.

_____

b He began to turn over more and more responsibility for his assistant.

_____

c She turned over to the rights to the product to a US company.

_____

d The job might have to be turned over by a more experienced person.

_____

→ Now check your answers in the key.

Build your vocabulary

SIMILAR VERBS → HAND SOMETHING OVER (TO SOMEBODY), HAND OVER (TO SOMEBODY) on page 44

99 wind something or itself up

Study Read these sentences carefully.

- Rising prices and falling sales have forced us to **wind up** the business.
- He was involved in **winding** the company **up**.
- The company's board voted against **winding** it **up**.
- Although the company was solvent, it decided to **wind** itself **up**.
- The trust could be **wound up** or merged with another bigger trust.

Check

Use the sentences in the Study box to help you do these exercises.

MEANING

Complete the meaning of this sense of **wind something up** by choosing the best words to fill the spaces.

If someone winds up a company or business they *close/expand/start* it *a little/completely/a lot*.

GRAMMAR

Which of these are grammatically correct?

a The business was wound up in 2004.
b The club was wound it up.
c The company had to wind itself up.
d They had to wind the business up.
e Falling sales forced them to wind up the business.

→ Now check your answers in the key.

Practise

1 Choose the correct form of the verb **wind up** for each sentence:

a Many businesses are being **wind up/wound up**.
b If negotiations fail, the company will be **winded up/wound up**.
c The organization was **wound up/been wound up** in 2003.

2 Complete the sentences with an appropriate form of **wind up**.

a The shipping group decided to _____ its final salary pension scheme.

b Under these circumstances, the UK plants may have to be _____ .

c The agency is attempting to _____ itself _____ in an orderly way.

d The decision to begin _____ the business was taken at a meeting of the main shareholders.

→ Now check your answers in the key.

Build your vocabulary

OTHER MEANINGS This verb can also be used with the same meaning but without an object:

- *The business went bankrupt and **wound up**.*
- *What happens to their benefits if their fund **winds up**?*

Wind something up or **wind up** can also be used to mean 'to bring an activity or meeting to an end'.

- *He **wound** the meeting **up** by wishing us a safe journey home.*
- *To **wind up**, I'd just like to remind you of a few points.*

100 write something off

Check

Use the sentences in the Study box to help you do these exercises.

MEANING

Which of these best matches this meaning of **write something off**?

a to write a cheque
b to accept that an amount of money has been lost or will not be paid
c to spend an amount of money to make a business profitable

GRAMMAR

Two of these sentences have a mistake. Find and correct them.

a They wrote off the debts.
b They wrote the debts off.
c They wrote off it.
d They wrote it off.
e The debts were written it off.

→ Now check your answers in the key.

Practise

1 Fill the gaps in these sentences using the correct form of **write something off**:

a The bank was forced to _____ the loan.

b It was a disastrous year in which the company _____ $270 million in investments.

c The losses had to be _____ .

2 Rewrite the words in italic so that the meaning stays the same, using a form of **write something off**.

a We decided to *accept that the loan would never be paid back.*

We _____

b The company can't recover its losses, so the directors *have accepted that they have lost $4 million.*

The company can't recover its losses, so the directors _____ .

→ Now check your answers in the key.

Build your vocabulary

RELATED WORDS NOUN: **write-off** (This is a countable noun.)

▸ *The company announced a further $300 million **write-off** last month.*

OTHER MEANINGS In accounting **write something off** means 'to reduce the value of an asset to nothing over a particular period of time' and is similar to **depreciate**:

▸ *Goodwill was **written off** over 5 years.*

In more general use, it means 'to decide that somebody or something is a failure or has no value'.

Key to exercises

1 ac'count for something
to form or be the source of a particular amount

Check
MEANING: c
GRAMMAR: a, c

Practise
1 **a** Students account for about 10% of our customers.
b 28% of jobs in the region are accounted for by manufacturing jobs. **2 a** Men accounted for 90% of managers in 1970. **b** Men account for 75% of managers in 2005. **c** Women accounted for 10% of managers in 1970.
d Women account for 25% of managers in 2005.

2 ˌback something 'up
to make a copy of a file, a program, etc. that can be used if the main one fails or needs extra support

Check
MEANING: b
GRAMMAR: a, b, d, e

Practise
1 **a** Have you backed the data up? *or* Have you backed up the data? **b** I backed it up on the hard drive. **c** I forgot to back it up. **2 a** … I hadn't *backed it up on the hard drive*.
b You can *back up all your folders* … *or* … *back all your folders up* … **c** *Backing up data* is … **d** … remember to *back up your work* on the C-drive. *or* … remember to *back your work up* on the C-drive.

3 ˌbail somebody or something 'out (of something)
to rescue sb/sth from difficulties, especially financial difficulties

Check
MEANING: rescue, difficulties, financial
GRAMMAR: a, b, c, e

Practise
1 **a** … the government usually *bails them out*.
b A millionaire fan has offered to *bail out the football club*.
c … the government will not *bail it out*. **d** The telecoms company was *bailed out by its shareholders*. **e** The state will not be able to go on *bailing out loss-making companies*.

4 ˌbeat 'off somebody or something
to defeat sb/sth in a competition

Check
MEANING: b
GRAMMAR: a, c, d NOTE You can also use the structure *beat the competition off* but this is less frequent.

Practise
1 **a** iv **b** i **c** iii **d** ii **2 a** beating off **b** beat off **c** beaten off

5 be 'down; be 'up
to be at a lower level or rate; to be at a higher level or rate

Check
MEANING: *Suggested Answers:* costs, productivity, shares, etc.
GRAMMAR: a, c, d, e

Practise
1 **a** are up **b** were down by **c** be up **d** is up **e** are down
2 a Profits in the airline industry are down by 7%.
b Company sales are up by 7%. **c** Share prices are down.

6 ˌbottom 'out
if markets, prices or bad situations **bottom out**, they reach their lowest point and then stop getting worse

Check
MEANING: lowest, worse
GRAMMAR: b

Practise
1 **a** the early 1950s **b** the mid-1970s **c** The baby boomers reached working age and the average family size fell.
2 a The share price *bottomed out* at $5.45. **b** Sales are *bottoming out*.

7 ˌbranch 'out (into something)
to begin to do a new job or an activity that you do not usually do

Check
MEANING: c
GRAMMAR: a, b, d

Practise
1 **a** branch out into **b** branch out **2 a** We have now *branched out into* sportswear. **b** … we decided to *branch out into* computer games. **c** … and I would like to *branch out on my own*.

8 ˌbreak 'down
to fail

Check
MEANING: c
GRAMMAR: b, e

Practise
1 **a** talks **b** deal **c** negotiations **2 a** broke down **b** break down **c** broke down. **d** breaking down **e** broke down **f** broken down

9 ˌbreak something 'down (into something)
to separate sth into smaller parts in order to analyse it or deal with it more easily

Check
MEANING: c
GRAMMAR: a, b, e NOTE **Break down** can also be used without an object when describing sth that can be separated into different parts: *The job breaks down into five main areas.*

Practise
1 **a** iv **b** i **c** iii **d** v **e** ii **2 a** … the manufacture of a car was **divided** into 84 simple tasks … **b** By **separating out** production in this way, … **a** … production is *broken down* into a few **simple** tasks. **b** Ford *broke down* the production of the Model T into 84 tasks. *or* … *broke* the production of the Model T *down* into …

10 ˌbreak 'into something
to start to get involved in an activity that it is difficult to become involved in and to be successful at it

Check
MEANING: 1 involved, industry, successful 2 a market, an industry, a career
GRAMMAR: a, b, d

Practise
1 **a** … and has already **broken** into … **b** … to break **into** the music business. **c** … we broke **into** the mass market with …
2 a … a tough task to *break into the budget travel market*.
b … but still couldn't *break into the restaurant business*.
c … but finally they *broke into the top ten companies*.
d … *broken into the toy industry*

11 ˌbreak something 'up; ˌbreak itself 'up
to divide sth into smaller parts; to be divided in this way

Check
MEANING: a

GRAMMAR: **b** The company was forced to *break itself up*. **d** The company was *broken up*. NOTE The pattern *break a company up* is possible, but rare.

Practise

1 a It was decided to *break up* the publishing department … **b** Businesses are often *broken up* into smaller units as … **c** The company has *broken* itself *up* into two separate businesses. **2** *Suggested Answers:* **a** Yes, but it has been broken up into several divisions. **b** Yes, he is going to break it up.

12 ˌbring something ˈforward
to move sth to an earlier date or time

Check
MEANING: **b**
GRAMMAR: **d** The meeting **was** brought forward.

Practise
Suggested Answers: **a** … but we *brought* it *forward* to Monday. *or* … it has been *brought forward* to … **b** Can't we *bring* it *forward* to 2 o'clock? **c** … if you can *bring* it *forward* by two weeks? **d** They have now *brought* it *forward* to March 17th.

13 ˌbring somebody ˈin
to ask sb to do a particular job or to be involved in sth, especially to help or advise

Check
MEANING: **c**
GRAMMAR: **a, b, d, e**

Practise
1 a We could *bring in a financial adviser. or* … *bring a financial adviser in.* **b** *A team of experts was brought in.* **c** It's time to *bring in an architect. or* … *bring an architect in.* **d** We should have *brought in a lawyer. or* … *brought a lawyer in.* **e** I heard they *had brought in a new managing director* to run it. *or* … *brought a new managing director in* … **f** I think she's planning *to bring in a partner. or* … *bring a partner in.* **2** *Suggested Answer:* Local firm brings in famous chefs to raise money for children. (*or* Celebrity chefs brought in to cook up some cash for the kids.)

14 ˌbring something ˈin; ˌbring something ˈinto something
to make or earn a particular amount of money

Check
MEANING: **a**
GRAMMAR: **b** The deal brought in $5 billion. NOTE This meaning of **bring in** is not usually used in the passive. The pattern **bring somebody in something** is also possible: *His job only brought him in a small income.*

Practise
1 a ii **b** i **c** iv **d** iii **2 a** bring in **b** brought in **c** bring in **d** brought in **e** brings in

15 ˌbring something ˈout
to produce or publish sth

Check
MEANING: **c**
GRAMMAR: **a, b, d**

Practise
1 a … **are** now bringing out new … **b** … when Fiat first brought it **out**. **2 a** The auto manufacturer *brought out* a new *model* of the car … **b** Magazine publishers are *bringing out* a range of *titles* that … **c** They will probably *bring out* an updated *version* of the software … **d** The model was not very successful when the company first *brought* it *out*.

16 ˌbring something ˈup
to mention a subject or start to talk about it

Check
MEANING: **a**
GRAMMAR: **a, b, d**

Practise
a OK. Can you *bring it up* at the next meeting? **b** You'd better *bring it up* with your manager. **c** No. I haven't *brought it up* yet. **d** Why didn't you *bring it up* earlier? **e** That was the first topic that *was brought up. or* ….that *she brought up*.

17 ˌbuild something ˈup
to create or develop sth

Check
MEANING: **c**
GRAMMAR: **a, b, c, e** NOTE The pattern *build sth up* is less frequent.

Practise
1 a It's important *to build up a good relationship* with your customers. **b** He has spent the last 10 years *building up a large group of clients*. **c** Each year fashion houses have to *build up new collections*. **d** … we have *built up a picture* of what customers want. **2 a** The company was gradually built up over 20 years. **b** Not all firms manage to build up a strong management team. **c** … if I wanted to be successful I must build up good contacts. **d** It didn't take her long to build up a reputation as an honest and reliable worker.

18 ˌburn ˈout; ˌburn yourself ˈout
to become extremely tired or sick/ill by working too hard over a period of time

Check
MEANING: **c**
GRAMMAR: **a, b**

Practise
1 a burn out *or* burn themselves out **b** burn out *or* burn themselves out **c** burning out *or* burning yourself out **d** burned/burnt out *or* burned/burnt themselves out **e** burned/burnt out *or* burned/burnt herself out

19 ˌbuy somebody or something ˈout
to buy part of a company, business, etc. from sb else, usually in order to get control of it

Check
MEANING: **b**
GRAMMAR: **a, b, c, e**

Practise
1 a I want to buy my partner out. *or* I want to buy out my partner. **b** The company has been bought out by a group of its employees. **2 a** bought out **b** buy out **c** buy *him* out **3 a** If you want to have complete control of the business, why don't you buy her out? **b** The fund has bought out (*the shares of*) the other investors at $101.50 a share.

20 ˌcall ˈback
to visit sb again for a particular purpose

Check
MEANING: the same, again
GRAMMAR: **a, d**

Practise
1 a iii **b** i **c** ii **2** *Suggested Answers:* **a** Can you call back after lunch? **b** I'll call back with the other document tomorrow. **c** I'll call back in three months to check it.

21 ˌcarry something ˈout
to do and complete a task

Check
MEANING: doing
GRAMMAR: a, b, c

Practise
1 **a** carry out **b** carried out **c** carry out **d** carried out
2 *Suggested Answers:* **a** The laboratory carries out *tests* each month. **b** An outside contractor is carrying out the *work*. **c** The *research* was carried out in secret. **d** The surveyor carried out an *inspection* of the building.

22 ‚cash 'in (on something)
to gain an advantage for yourself from a situation

Check
MEANING: c
GRAMMAR: a, d

Practise
1 **a** ii **b** iv **c** i **d** iii 2 **a** The banks have *cashed in on …*
b … and many companies have been *cashing in*. **c** … and several TV companies are trying to *cash in on* them.

23 ‚catch 'on
(used about a product or an idea) to become popular with people

Check
MEANING: b
GRAMMAR: a, b, d

Practise
1 **a** Broadband is really catching on. *or* Broadband has really caught on. **b** Camera phones haven't caught on with older people. **c** Electronic greetings cards have caught on. **d** … people thought that duvets wouldn't catch on in the UK. 2 *Suggested Answers:* **a** Jogging really caught on in the 1980s. **b** Video phones haven't really caught on yet but they may do soon.

24 ‚clean something 'up
to remove crime and immoral behaviour from a place or an activity

Check
MEANING: improve, removing, dishonest
GRAMMAR: a, b, d, e NOTE The pattern *clean the industry up* is possible but less frequent.

Practise
a cleaning up **b** cleaning up **c** clean it up **d** cleans up **e** be cleaned up

25 ‚close something 'down; ‚close 'down
if a shop/store, business, etc. **closes down**, or sb **closes it down**, it stops operating as a business, usually permanently

Check
MEANING: b
GRAMMAR: a, b, c

Practise
1 **a** to close down **b** closed down **c** close it down 2 **a** to close down **b** closed down **c** to close it down

26 ‚contract something 'out (to somebody)
to arrange for work to be done by another company or by sb outside your company

Check
MEANING: arrange, work, another company, your own
GRAMMAR: a, b, d

Practise
1 **a** Taylor Trucks **b** No **c** A&B have reduced their costs significantly. 2 **a** The company *contracts out* its advertising. *or* … *contracts* its advertising *out*. **b** We *contract out* the office cleaning. *or* We *contract* the office cleaning *out*.

27 ‚copy somebody 'in (on something)
to make sure that sb receives a copy of a letter, an electronic message, etc. that you are sending to sb else

Check
MEANING: b
GRAMMAR: a, c, d

Practise
1 **a** Can you copy me in on the email? **b** I copy him in on all my correspondence. **c** It is important to copy her in on all emails. 2 **a** Would you like me to *copy you in* when …? **b** It is essential to *copy your secretary in* on all correspondence. **c** Why didn't you *copy me in on the report*?

28 ‚cut 'back (on something); ‚cut something 'back
to reduce sth such as the amount sb spends or produces

Check
MEANING: d
GRAMMAR: a, b, d, e

Practise
1 **a** A lot of firms had to cut back ~~on~~ during the recession. **b** Expenditure on essential services will not be cut ~~it~~ back. **c** Consumers cut back on ~~it~~ their borrowing in November. 2 **a** … must *cut back on* spending. **b** … *will be cut back* in the next few years. **c** … we *cut back on* staff. **d** The funding for this project *has been cut back* dramatically.

29 'deal with something
to take action to solve a problem, carry out a task, etc., especially as part of your job

Check
MEANING: c
GRAMMAR: a, c, d

Practise
1 **a** deal with **b** dealing with **c** deal with **d** dealt with 2 **a** We need to *deal with* the *situation* … **b** The *matter* will be *dealt with* by … **c** My job involves *dealing with complaints* from customers. **d** He … asked me to *deal with it*.

30 dis'pose of something
to sell part of a business, property, etc.

Check
MEANING: sell, asset, shares
GRAMMAR: a, c, d

Practise
1 **a** disposed of **b** disposed of **c** dispose of **d** disposing of.
2 **a** Disposing of **b** dispose of **c** disposed of **d** dispose of **e** disposed of

31 ‚draw something 'up
to make or write sth that needs careful thought or planning

Check
MEANING: write, document
GRAMMAR: a, c, d, e NOTE The pattern *draw a plan up* is possible but less frequent.

Practise
1 **a** … to *draw up* the *document* … **b** She is busy *drawing up* a *contract* … **c** The committee has *drawn up* some new *rules*. **d** I'll *draw up* a *list* of people … 2 **a** We're drawing up some new guidelines. **b** I need to draw up a report for my boss. **c** The contract was drawn up last year. **d** The company is drawing up plans for a new project.

32 ‚drop 'off
to decrease in level or amount, especially after being high for a long time

Check

MEANING: c
GRAMMAR: a, d

Practise

1 a Profits … are expected to *drop off* in the next six months.
b Demand for the product has *dropped off* although …
c Sales usually increase around January and *drop off* …
d We expect our profits to *drop off* as … 2 a The number of
customers has *dropped off sharply/dramatically/noticeably*.
b Auto sales continued to *drop off sharply/dramatically/
noticeably* in the winter. c … after foreign business *dropped
off sharply/dramatically/ noticeably*.

33 ˌdrum 'up something

to try hard to get support or business

Check

MEANING: 1 a 2 c
GRAMMAR: a, c, d NOTE You can also use the pattern *drum
more business up* but this is rare.

Practise

1 a … and *(to) drum up new business or* … *drumming up*
b They need to *drum up cash* to pay off … c … a TV
advertising campaign to *drum up interest* in the new brand.
d … new ways of *drumming up customers*. e The lower entry
price has *drummed up more visitors* for … 2 *Suggested
Answers:* I could drum up business by posting leaflets to
possible customers, placing an ad in the local newspaper, etc.

34 ˌdry 'up

if a supply of sth dries up, there is gradually less of it until
there is none left

Check

MEANING: supply, gradually, less, none
GRAMMAR: a

Practise

1 a Work has dried up. b Orders from abroad could dry up
at any time. c Demand for our products is drying up. or …
has started to dry up. 2 *Suggested Answers:* a Sales started
to dry up in 1998. b Sales almost dried up completely in
2003. c After almost drying up in 2003, sales started to
improve in 2004.

35 ˌfactor something 'in; ˌfactor something 'into something

to include a particular fact or situation when you are
calculating sth, thinking about sth or planning sth

Check

MEANING: c
GRAMMAR: e These costs are factored **into** their
calculations. NOTE The pattern *factor costs in* is possible but
not very frequent.

Practise

1 a in b into c in d into 2 a … *has been factored into* our
calculations. b It is important *to factor in* interest payments
… c The cost of materials *should be factored in* when …

36 ˌfall 'through

to fail to be completed; to not happen

Check

MEANING: b
GRAMMAR: a, c, d

Practise

1 a Twice (= 2 times) b The union refused to accept the
extra money offered by the management. c Because they
cannot agree over the question of sick pay. 2 a fall through
b fallen through c fall through d fell through e fell through

37 ˌfill somebody 'in (on something)

to tell sb about sth that has happened

Check

MEANING: c
GRAMMAR: c Has James been filled **in** on what's
happened? NOTE The pattern *fill in James on what's
happened* is very rare.

Practise

1 a I will fill you in on the news. b She filled me in on what
happened. c Can you fill me in on the details of the
meeting? 2 a iii b iv c i d ii 3 a Yes, Alan's filled me in.
b Yes, I'll ask the sales manager to fill you in.

38 ˌfill 'in for somebody

to do sb's job for a short time while they are not there

Check

MEANING: job, short, away
GRAMMAR: a, b

Practise

1 a Can someone *fill in for him*? b Who's going to *fill in for
me* …? c I'm just *filling in for a secretary* who is in hospital.
d Thank you for *filling in for Joy* and … 2 a Temporary
workers are doing the work normally done by the workers
who are on strike. b Grandmothers are looking after the
children while their parents are at work.

39 ˌfirm 'up something

if sb **firms up** an arrangement, an agreement, etc. it
becomes more definite or less likely to change

Check

MEANING: b
GRAMMAR: c The details have been discussed but we need
to firm **them** up. NOTE You can also use the pattern *firm the
arrangements up* but this is rare.

Practise

1 a firmed up b firming up c firm it up d will firm up e firm
up 2 *Suggested Answers:* a Yes, we are firming them up
now. b No, it has not been firmed up yet.

40 'focus on something

to give all your attention, effort, etc. to a particular
problem, subject or person

Check

MEANING: b
GRAMMAR: a, b NOTE The spellings *focused/focusing* and
focussed/focussing are both used. This verb is not used in the
passive.

Practise

1 a ii b iv c i d iii 2 a It needs *to focus on* increasing
profits. b The meeting *will focus on* recruitment of staff.
c The report *focuses on* staff development. d The research
focused on the problems faced by small businesses.

41 ˌgo 'down; ˌgo 'up

to become lower or smaller; to become higher or larger

Check

MEANING: *Suggested Answers:* taxes, income, interest rates
GRAMMAR: a, b, d, e

Practise

1 a Prices are expected to *go up*. b The yen has *gone down* in
value by 5%. c Inflation is *going down*. d We are trying to
prevent our costs from *going up*. 2 *Suggested Answers:* a
Income tax has gone down. b Inflation is expected to go up
by 2%.

42 ˌgo 'under

to fail, lose power, etc.; to be unable to pay what you owe

Check
MEANING: c
GRAMMAR: a, e

Practise
1 a ii b v c i d iv e iii 2 *Suggested Answers:* a … more and more companies are going under. b … until it went under. c If spending levels do not increase soon, we will go under. d Several small companies in the town have gone under since the recession began. e If you don't keep up with technology, you will go under.

43 ˌhammer 'out something

to discuss a plan or a deal for a long time and with great effort, until sth is decided or agreed on

Check
MEANING: discuss, long, great, details, agreed
GRAMMAR: a, c, d NOTE The pattern *hammer a deal out* is possible but rare.

Practise
1 a hammer out b hammered out c hammered out d hammer out 2 *Suggested Answers:* a … to *hammer out* a *rescue package.* b … because we haven't *hammered out* the *marketing strategy* yet. c No, I'm still *hammering out* the *final details.*

44 ˌhand something 'over (to somebody); ˌhand 'over (to somebody)

to give sb else your position of power or the responsibility for sth

Check
MEANING: a
GRAMMAR: a, b, c, e

Practise
1 a handed over b hand over c handed over 2 *Suggested Answers:* b He has *handed over responsibility* for the project to his assistant. c She is *handing over the director's job* to her successor next month.

45 ˌhead 'up something

to lead or be in charge of a department, part of an organization, etc.

Check
MEANING: b
GRAMMAR: a, b, c NOTE The pattern *head the department up* is very rare.

Practise
1 a False: Bob Eyre heads up the sales team. b True c True d False: The IT department is headed up by Joan Carr. 2 a to head up b to head up c be headed up d heads up

46 ˌhire something or somebody 'out

to allow sb to use sth for a short period of time in return for payment; to arrange for sb or yourself to work for sb else

Check
MEANING: b
GRAMMAR: c The company hires **them** out.

Practise
1 a Adams Autos hires out cars. b Camden Catering Company hire out catering staff. c Thames Temps hire out temporary secretarial and office staff. 2 a … there are several companies that *hire out both Apple Macs and PCs.* b She *hires herself out as* … c We *hire out cameras* to film companies. d Our company *hires out interpreters* for …

47 ˌhold 'up

to remain strong

Check
MEANING: c
GRAMMAR: b, d

Practise
1 … our profits *have remained solid* … the euro *kept its value* against the dollar …, demand for our goods has *continued at the same level* … 2 a holding up b hold up c held up d held up e held up 3 a holding up b held up c holding up

48 ˌhook something or somebody 'up (to something)

to connect sth/sb to a piece of electronic equipment or to a power supply

Check
MEANING: connect, electrical, equipment, supply
GRAMMAR: a, b, c, e

Practise
1 a up to b it up c up to 2 a We don't have enough cables *to hook up all the computers.* b … Do you mind if I *hook it up?* c … this machine *isn't hooked up to* a printer. d We have eighteen computers *hooked up to* the Internet. e I heard he had *hooked up a tape recorder to his telephone* so …

49 ˌhook 'up (with somebody)

to start working with sb

Check
MEANING: a
GRAMMAR: a, b

Practise
1 a They have hooked ~~it~~ up with … b The two companies hooked up ~~with~~ in order to combine their expertise. c … when they ~~were~~ hooked up last year. 2 a hooking up with b to hook up with c hooked up d hooked up with e to hook up

50 ˌkey something 'in; ˌkey something 'into something

to put information into a computer using a keyboard

Check
MEANING: information, keyboard
GRAMMAR: a She keyed *it in.* b She keyed *the data* into the computer. c She keyed *it* into the computer. d The data was keyed *into* the computer.

Practise
1 a iv b iii c ii d i 2 a Can you *key this data into* the computer? b … you may have *keyed it into* the database wrongly. c … you can now *key in* a four-figure PIN instead of …

51 ˌlay somebody 'off

to stop employing sb because there is not enough work for them to do

Check
MEANING: b
GRAMMAR: a, b, d

Practise
1 a True b False c True 2 a The company will have to *lay off* 150 workers if … b He *was laid off* when … c They *laid off* half the workforce due to … d We are hoping to avoid closing plants and *laying off* staff *or laying staff off.*

52 ˌlay something 'out

to spend money on sth

Check

MEANING: c
GRAMMAR: a, b, c NOTE The pattern *lay money out* is possible but rare.

Practise

1 a laid out b lay out c been laid out d laying out e will lay out

53 ˌlevel 'off

to become level or steady after a period of sharp rises or falls

Check

MEANING: 1 c 2 c
GRAMMAR: c Prices have started to level off now.

Practise

1 A 2003 B 2003 C 2005 2 a Graph A: rose, 2003, levelled off b Graph B: fell, levelled off c Graph C: 2005, fell and then levelled off.

54 ˌlock somebody, something or yourself 'into something; ˌlock somebody, something or yourself 'in

to involve sb, sth or yourself in a situation that cannot easily be changed

Check

MEANING: a True b True c False
GRAMMAR: a, b, d NOTE *Lock in/into* is most frequently used in the passive e.g. *He was locked into the contract for four years.*

Practise

1 a to lock herself into b be locked into c lock it into d locked him into 2 a ... that their money *is locked into* very long-term investments. b No, if you don't want to *lock in* your money for that length of time, ...

55 ˌmark something 'up

to increase the price of sth

Check

MEANING: b
GRAMMAR: a, b, d NOTE *Mark up* is often used in the passive. The pattern *mark the goods up* is possible but less frequent than *mark up the goods*.

Practise

1 a iii b i c ii 2 a mark up *prices* b mark up *their beds* c marking up *drinks*

56 ˌmeasure 'up (to/against something)

to be as good, successful, etc. as expected or needed

Check

MEANING: b
GRAMMAR: a, c, d

Practise

1 a to b well c against d measuring 2 a Drivers who *do not measure up* could be fired. b How does your firm *measure up* to the best? c She was trying *to measure up to* her parents, ... d Many companies have failed *to measure up to* the challenges they face. e How *do* your staff *measure up*?

57 ˌmount 'up

to increase gradually in size and quantity

Check

MEANING: 1 c 2 *Suggested Answers:* bills, expenses, paperwork
GRAMMAR: a, c, d

Practise

a Our bills are *mounting up* at an alarming rate. b Fuel costs were really starting to *mount up*. c The legal fees *mounted up* and ... d As the debt *mounts up*, so too ... e The paperwork soon *mounts up* if ... f Her unpaid fines have *mounted up* and ... g The bank said the losses had begun to *mount up* in 1997.

58 ˌopen 'up; ˌopen something 'up

FIRST MEANING
to become or make sth possible, available or able to be reached

Check

MEANING: b
GRAMMAR: a, c, d NOTE The pattern *open markets up* is quite rare.

Practise

1 a opening up b open up c been opened up d open up e opens up f open up g opening up 2 *Suggested Answers:* a ii *The Internet* has opened up *a wider market* to many companies. b iii *The reforms* will open up *new job opportunities* in this sector. c i *Telecom operators* have been forced to open up *their networks* to other companies.

59 ˌopen 'up; ˌopen 'up something

SECOND MEANING
to start a new business

Check

MEANING: start
GRAMMAR: a, c, d NOTE The pattern *open a new store up* is rare.

Practise

1 a open up b opened up c opening up d opened up
2 a How many *new banks opened up* in the town last year? b There are plans for a motorbike factory to *open up* here in 2010. c ... they *opened up* (*or had opened up*) new offices in Tokyo a few years ago. d Are they going *to open up a new store* here soon?

60 ˌpay something 'back (to somebody); ˌpay somebody 'back

to return money that you borrowed from sb

Check

MEANING: c
GRAMMAR: c The company paid **them** back. NOTE In informal language *pay sb back sth* and, less often, *pay sb sth back* are also used: *When are you going to pay me back that $100 you owe me? Can you pay me that money back soon?*

Practise

1 The company paid back debts of $3 million. 2 a pay us back b paying back c didn't pay the loan back d pay the money back

61 ˌpay 'up; ˌpay 'up something

to pay all the money that you owe to sb, especially when you do not want to or when the payment is late

Check

MEANING: pay, money, owe
GRAMMAR: a, c, d NOTE The pattern *pay the money up* is not possible. *He paid it up* and *he paid it up* are also not possible. You must say either *He paid up the money* or *He paid up.*

Practise

1 a pay up b paying up c pay up d paid up 2 *Suggested Answers:* a Yes, it's all paid up. b Yes, they paid up in full immediately. c No, and they say they'll cut off the phone if she doesn't pay up.

62 ˌpencil something or somebody 'in

to write down sb's name for an appointment, or details of an arrangement, although you know that this might have to be changed later

Check
MEANING: b
GRAMMAR: a, b, d NOTE The form *to pencil a date in* is less usual than *to pencil in a date*. *Pencil in* is used more frequently in British English than in American English

Practise
1 a pencilled in b pencil you in c pencilled in

63 ˌphase something 'out

to stop using sth gradually in stages over a period of time

Check
MEANING: gradually, stages
GRAMMAR: b The company phased it out. d The system was phased out.

Practise
1 a The company plans to phase out children's clothes. c The train company plans to phase out first class seats over the next two years. 2 a You can't *phase out a completely new product!* b ... and there are plans to *phase it out.* c ... and *700 jobs in the UK will be phased out.* d ... and *nuclear power (could be) phased out.*

64 ˌpick 'up

to get better, stronger, etc.; to improve

Check
MEANING: c
GRAMMAR: b Sales picked up.

Practise
1 In 2004, the company made *$6.5 million* but in 2005 sales *picked up* and the company made profits of *$7.2 million.*
2 a ii b iv c i d iii 3 a Unless passenger numbers *pick up* we ... b Business has *picked up* since ... c We're hoping that exports will *pick up* next year. d Sales are *picking up* thanks to ...

65 ˌprop something 'up

to help or support sth that is having difficulties

Check
MEANING: financial, money
GRAMMAR: a, b, d

Practise
1 a Badly b the staff pension fund c no 2 a They had to offer discounts to *prop up sales.* b ... profitable divisions are *propping up failing ones.* c ... farmers rely on their governments to *prop them up.* d State industries are sometimes *propped up* by ...

66 ˌpull 'out; ˌpull 'out of something

to stop being involved in sth or decide not to do sth you had promised to do

Check
MEANING: b, c
GRAMMAR: a, b

Practise
1 a One US airline *pulled out* of Sweden ... b ... our partners may decide to *pull out.* c ... but *pulled out* at the last minute. d The decision to *pull out* of the deal follows ...
2 *Suggested Answer:* The offer they received was rejected by their shareholders.

67 ˌput something 'in

to officially make a claim, request, etc.

Check
MEANING: 1 request, claim 2 bid
GRAMMAR: a, b, d

Practise
1 a Our company intends *to put in a bid for the contract.* b ... work involved in *putting in a patent application.* c He has *put in a claim for expenses.* 2 a Yes, they *put in an application* last week. b You have to *put in a request* to your line manager. c Yes, someone *put in an offer* in last week.

68 ˌput something to'gether

to create or prepare sth

Check
MEANING: 1 b 2 a
GRAMMAR: a, b, d, e

Practise
a Managers have *put together a deal* worth $25 million. b We are *putting together a group* of experts to ... c We *put together* our sales *force* in ... d Jack was the one who ... *put together* the *operation.* e The *video* has been *put together* as ...

69 ˌput 'up something

to provide or lend money

Check
MEANING: b
GRAMMAR: a, c, d NOTE The pattern *put money up* is possible but is used less frequently than *put up money*.

Practise
1 a iv b i c ii d iii 2 a ... they must put up the cash. b ... if another organization puts up the other half. c Cigarette companies have been asked to put up the funding ...

70 reˌport 'back

to give sb information about sth that they have asked you to find out about

Check
MEANING: information
GRAMMAR: a, d, e

Practise
1 a ... *report back with* our results. b He *reported back that* ... c I need to *report back to* ... d I'll *report back on* the meeting. e ... she *reported back to* ... 2 *Suggested Answers:* I have to attend a meeting on March 9 and report back to James.
3 *Suggested Answers:* Hi. There is a conference I would like you to attend from June 12th to June 14th in Dallas. I can't make it so could you go there and then report back to me about it. Many thanks, Lee.

71 reˈport to somebody

if you **report to** sb in a company or an organization, they are responsible for your work and tell you what to do

Check
MEANING: responsible, work, tell
GRAMMAR: a, b, d

Practise
Suggested Answers: f Jack Daniels ..., reporting to Joan Carr.

72 ˌrip somebody 'off

to cheat sb, for example by making them pay too much or by selling them sth of poor quality

Check
MEANING: cheat, too much, poor
GRAMMAR: a, b, c, e NOTE *Rip off* is more common in British English than American English. It is often used in the

passive: *I was ripped off.*

Practise
1 a … ripping her off. **b** … rip them off. **c** … ripping you off *or* ripped off. **d** ripped them off. **2** *Suggested Answers:* **a** You were ripped off! **b** Yes, they really ripped him off. **c** We were totally ripped off.

73 ,roll something 'out
to introduce a new product, service or technology by gradually making it available to more people NOTE Roll out can also mean *to show a new aircraft or vehicle to the public for the first time.* For example: *It will be the world's biggest passenger airline when they roll it out in 2006.*

Check
MEANING: **b**
GRAMMAR: **a, b, d, e**

Practise
1 The company **rolled** out its new product last month. **b** … but we hope to roll it **out** by the end of the year. **c** The car company rolled **out** a $15 million ad campaign …
2 a The service will *be rolled out* commercially … **b** Before *rolling out* a new product … *or* Before *rolling* a new product *out* … **c** … and then *roll it out* to other regions next year. **d** The group *rolled its new car out* on Thursday. *or* … *rolled out its new car* …

74 ,round something 'up (to something)
to increase a number to the next highest whole number

Check
MEANING: less, increasing, highest
GRAMMAR: **a, b, c, e** NOTE The pattern *round the price up* is less common than *round up the price.*

Practise
1 a 25 **b** 88 **c** 107 **2 a** the change from national currencies to the euro **b** by rounding prices up rather than down **c** small food stores, restaurants and cafes **3 a** rounded up **b** rounded up **c** round up

75 ,rule something or somebody 'out (as something); ,rule something or somebody 'out of something
to state or decide that sth is not possible or that sb/sth is not suitable

Check
MEANING: **c**
GRAMMAR: **a, b, d, e** NOTE The pattern *rule job cuts out* is possible but rare.

Practise
1 a been **b** them **c** of **d** itself **2 a** No, the union has *ruled out the possibility* of a strike. **b** No, both sides have *ruled out a merger*. **c** … as the company *has not ruled out further job losses* …

76 ,run something 'by/'past somebody
to show sb sth or tell sb about an idea in order to see their reaction to it

Check
MEANING: tell, opinion
GRAMMAR: **a, c, d, e**

Practise
1 a … *run it past* my line manager … **b** She *ran the figures by* the sales team … **c** Do you mind if I *run some suggestions by* you …? **d** I was nervous about *running my business plan past* the bank manager. **2** *Suggested Answers:* **a** In order to run my company accounts past him. **b** I want to run an idea by you. **c** I was running some slogans by him to see which ones he liked.

77 ,run 'up something
to allow a bill, debt, etc. to reach a large total

Check
MEANING: **1** owe **2** a debt, costs, a deficit, a bill
GRAMMAR: **a, b, d** NOTE The pattern *run a bill up* is rare.

Practise
1 a ran up **b** run up **c** run up **d** running up **2 a** *Suggested Answers:* It could run up large debts by spending too much on new equipment, taking over other businesses, etc.

78 ,sell something 'off
to sell all or part of an industry, a company, etc. often at a low price in order to get rid of it

Check
MEANING: **c**
GRAMMAR: **a, b, d** NOTE The pattern *sell a business off* is less common than *sell off a business.*

Practise
1 a sold off **b** sell off **c** sold it off **d** sell the division off **e** sold off

79 ,set something 'up
to arrange for sth to happen

Check
MEANING: **d**
GRAMMAR: **d** Helen set **it** up.

Practise
a … I'll *set up an interview* for you *or* … *set an interview* up … **b** I think we should *set up a meeting* to discuss … *or* … *set a meeting* up … **c** My assistant is responsible for *setting up my appointments or* … *setting my appointments* up. **d** Thanks to everyone involved in *setting it up*. **e** I'll *set up the transport arrangements or* … *set the transport arrangements* up **f** We've *set up a talk* for … *or* … *set a talk up* …

80 ,shake something or somebody 'up
to make important changes in an organization, a profession, etc. in order to make it more efficient

Check
MEANING: **c**
GRAMMAR: **a** The new manager should shake **it** up. **c** The new manager should shake ~~it~~ up the business.

Practise
1 a v **b** ii **c** iv **d** iii **e** i

81 ,shop a'round; ,shop a'round something
to compare the quality or prices of goods or services that are offered by different shops/stores, companies, etc. so that you can choose the best

Check
MEANING: **c**
GRAMMAR: **a, c**

Practise
1 a shops **b** to **c** for **d** find **e** best/lowest/cheapest **2 a** shopping around **b** shop around **c** shop around **d** shopped around **3 a** Customers should shop around for the best insurance deal. **b** Buying a new car? No need to shop around. Our prices are lowest!

82 ,sign 'up; ,sign somebody 'up
to arrange to receive or do sth; to arrange for sb to receive or do sth

Check
MEANING: **a, b, c**
GRAMMAR: **a, b, c, d**

Practise
1 a ... they are very keen to *sign him up*. b ... so I *signed up for* ... c The company has *signed up* over 2 000 customers ... d ... she *signed up with* a temping agency. e ... people will want to *sign up for* the free email service.

83 ˌsmarten something or somebody 'up
to make yourself, another person or a place look neater or more attractive

Check
MEANING: more attractive, cleaner, neater
GRAMMAR: a, b, c, e

Practise
1 a She will have to smarten herself **up** ... b ... but we've smartened **it** up now. c They have asked all their staff to smarten **up their** appearance. 2 a Yes, we definitely need to *smarten it up*. b It could easily be *smartened up*. c A lot of money needs to be spent on *smartening it up* to attract tourists again.

84 ˌstart 'up; ˌstart something 'up
to start operating or trading; to establish a business

Check
MEANING: c
GRAMMAR: a, b, d NOTE The pattern *start sth up* is less common than *start up sth*.

Practise
a They used the loan to *start up a new business of their own*. b A young journalist has *started up a free newspaper* in the town. c ... organizations that can offer you advice on how to *start up your own company*. d ... now I'm *starting one up*. e ... and *started up on her own*. f ... when we *start up on the Web*. g Many new insurance ventures have *started up since September*. h The airline is *starting up its second UK base* at Bournemouth.

85 ˌstep 'down (as / from something)
to leave an important job or position and let somebody else take your place

Check
MEANING: c
GRAMMAR: a, b, d

Practise
1 a as b as c from 2 a stepped down b step down c stepping down. d stepped down e step down

86 ˌstock 'up (on/with something)
to buy a lot of something so that you can use it later

Check
MEANING: a
GRAMMAR: a, c, e

Practise
1 a We need to stock up ~~for~~ on/with flowers to meet the huge demand. b ... so bookstores stocked ~~it~~ up on it. c He is going to use the money to stock up ~~of~~ on new products. 2 a Shoppers are already *stocking up* on *warm clothes* for the winter. b ... so the supermarkets *stocked up* on *cold drinks*. c Stores are starting to *stock up* for *the holiday season*. d Some shops *stock up* every day. e Some stores never *stock up* on *inventory* unless ...

87 ˌtake 'off
(about a product, an idea, etc.) to become successful or popular very quickly or suddenly

Check
MEANING: successful, popular
GRAMMAR: a, b, d

Practise
1 a It started off as a small company, but ~~was~~ has really taken off now. b His career really ~~taking~~ took off when he moved to the States. c Job-sharing started to take ~~on~~ off in the 1990s. 2 a Sales have *taken off* ... b The idea *took off* ... c He expects the business to *take off* ... d This type of insurance policy never really *took off* ... e There is no sign of our new product *taking off* ...

88 ˌtake somebody 'on
to employ sb

Check
MEANING: c
GRAMMAR: a, b, d, e

Practise
1 a iii b iv c ii d i 2 a The company usually *takes on* quite a lot of students during the summer. b Firms are now much more willing to *take on* disabled people. c ... but they didn't *take me on*. d ... she was *taken on* as an area manager.

89 ˌtake somebody or something 'on
to compete or fight against somebody

Check
MEANING: compete, fight, more
GRAMMAR: a, b, c

Practise
1 a No other software company has yet *taken on the market leader*. b ... now we *are taking them* on. c New bargain superstores are ... *taking on the traditional chain stores*. d The company ... believes that it can *take on the competition*. e She decided to *take on her former employers* and ... 2 *Suggested Answers*: a Somebody took legal action against a major airline *or* a small airline tried to compete against them for business. b The government has promised to take action against large companies that create pollution.

90 ˌtake something 'on
to decide to do something; to agree to be responsible for something

Check
MEANING: b
GRAMMAR: a, b, d

Practise
1 a ... *not to take on too much work*. b ... no-one else was willing to *take on this task*. c Whoever *takes on sales and marketing* should ... d Our firm has never *taken on such a big project* before. e She is *taking on an extra day's work* to help pay the bills. f ... willing to *take on his case*. g There has been an increase in ... *part-time work taken on* by students.

91 ˌtake something 'over
to gain control of a company, especially by buying shares

Check
MEANING: c
GRAMMAR: c They will take over the company.

Practise
1 a iv b i c ii d iii 2 a take over b taking over c taken over d taken over e took *it* over

92 take over (from somebody) (as something); take something over (from somebody)
to begin to have control of or responsibility for something, especially in place of somebody else

Check
MEANING: c

109

GRAMMAR: a, b, d

Practise

1 a Ms Camus *will* take over the post next week. **b** ... since he took over *as* CEO last March. **c** The new boss only took over ~~from~~ control a few weeks ago. **d** ... We'll need somebody special to take ~~you~~ over (*from you*). **2 a** Who is going *to take over from* Sam ...? **b** Who is going *to take over* Sam's job ...? **c** Amy *took over as* sales manager ... **d** He has made a lot of money since *taking over* the family business. **e** He *takes over/is taking over/ will take over* the running of the company next week.

93 ,tie something 'up

FIRST MEANING
to deal with all the remaining details of something

Check
MEANING: c
GRAMMAR: a, c, d, e NOTE The pattern *tie a deal up* is possible but not common.

Practise

1 a ... that the deal will be *completed* ... **b** ... that the financial arrangements can be *sorted out*. **2 a** tie up **b** tied up **c** tie up **d** tying up

94 ,tie something 'up (in something)

SECOND MEANING
to invest money so that it is not easily available for use

Check
MEANING: invest
GRAMMAR: a, b, c

Practise

1 a tied up **b** tie up **c** tied up **2** *Suggested Answers:* **a** All my money *is tied up in* property. **b** Its assets *are tied up in* raw materials. **c** I have *tied up* all my capital *in* my business. **d** They might be *tying up too much cash* ...

95 ,turn something a'round; ,turn a'round

if a business, an economy, etc. **turns around** or somebody **turns** it **around**, it starts being successful after it has failed to be successful for a time

Check
MEANING: c
GRAMMAR: a, b, d, e, f

Practise

Suggested Answers: **a** ... his experience in *turning around failing businesses or* ... *turning failing businesses around.* **b** The car maker is struggling to *turn around* its *falling European car sales*. **c** *The business was turned around* by ... **d** *The job market* hasn't *turned around* yet ... **e** You can no longer *turn around a struggling company* by ... *or* ... *turn a struggling company around* ...

96 ,turn 'down

to become weaker or less active, make less money, etc.

Check
MEANING: a weaker, less **b** decrease
GRAMMAR: a, e

Practise

1 a ... sales have fallen and *profits* have *turned down*. **b** The *market* for this type of product has *turned down* recently. **c** The government now fears that the *economy* may be beginning to *turn down*. **2 a** ... the economy is beginning to ~~become weaker~~ turn down. **b** Demand in some key markets such as housing has ~~declined~~ turned down, ... **c** ... many businesses have seen their sales and profits ~~decrease~~ turn down ...

97 ,turn something 'out

to produce something

Check
MEANING: c
GRAMMAR: a, b, d

Practise

1 a iv **b** iii **c** ii **d** v **e** i **2 a** The factory *turns out* a variety of medical devices. **b** The plant used to *turn out* 650 engines per day. **c** Analysts are expecting the company to *turn out* a ... ¥5 billion ... **d** The operation is currently *turning out* 800 000 barrels a day. **e** Most of our revenue lies in *turning out* paper ...

98 ,turn something 'over to somebody

to give the control of sth to sb else

Check
MEANING: give
GRAMMAR: a, b, d

Practise

1 a turn over **b** turned over **c** turning over **d** turns over **2 a** She turned ~~up~~ over a share of ... **b** He began to turn over more and more responsibility ~~for~~ to his assistant. **c** She turned over ~~to~~ the rights ... **d** The job might have to be turned over ~~by~~ to a more experienced person.

99 ,wind something or itself 'up

to stop running a business and close it completely

Check
MEANING: close, completely
GRAMMAR: a, c, d, e

Practise

1 a wound up **b** wound up **c** wound up **2 a** wind up **b** wound up **c** wind *itself* up **d** winding up

100 ,write something 'off

to remove a debt from a company's accounts because the money cannot be collected; to remove an asset that has no value

Check
MEANING: b
GRAMMAR: c They wrote **it** off. **e** The debts were written ~~it~~ off.

Practise

1 a write off **b** wrote off **c** written off **2 a** We decided to *write off the loan or* ... write *the loan* off **b** The company can't recover its losses, so the directors *have written off $4 million. or have written $4 million off.*